easy
Web Pages,
Second Edition

See it done

Do it yourself

que®

Part 1: Getting a Web Page Authoring Tool

Part 2: Building Your First Web Page   Pg. 12-27

Part 3: Making Your Page Say What You Want   Pg. 30-49

Part 4: Making Links   Pg. 50-67

Part 5: Adding Style to Your Pages   Pg. 68-93

Part 6: Creating Tables and Forms   Pg. 94-107

Part 7: Publishing Your Page Online   Pg. 108-123

Part 8: Announcing Your Page   Pg. 124-133

Part 9: Super Editing: HTML   Pg. 134-145

Part 10: Discovering Other Web Authoring Tools and Techniques Pg. 146-157

Part ▶ **1: Getting a Web Page Authoring Tool**

1 — Do You Already *Have* a Web-Authoring Tool?
2 — Surfing to Microsoft's Web Site to Get an Authoring Tool
3 — Downloading the Setup Program
4 — Installing Internet Explorer and FrontPage Express
5 — Opening FrontPage Express
6 — Discovering FrontPage Express's Toolbars

 Part ▶ **2: Building Your First Web Page**

1 — Starting the Personal Home Page Wizard
2 — Choosing What to Include on the Page
3 — Naming the Page and Its File
4 — Choosing the Style for Your List of Links
5 — Choosing the Information About You to Include
6 — Putting Contact Information at the Bottom of Your Page
7 — Choosing How to Receive Feedback from Your Visitors
8 — Choosing the Order of Information on Your Page
9 — Producing the Web Page
10 — Saving the New Page
11 — Closing and Re-Opening a Page File
12 — Opening a Web Page You Haven't Used Lately
13 — Changing Your Web Page Title
14 — Starting a Completely Blank Page
15 — Checking Out Your New Page in a Web Browser

 Part ▶ **3: Making Your Page Say What You Want**

1 — Selecting Text
2 — Changing Text on a Page
3 — Typing New Text
4 — Typing Symbols and Special Characters
5 — Deleting Text
6 — Fixing Mistakes
7 — Copying Text
8 — Moving Text
9 — Choosing the Style of a Paragraph
10 — Indenting a Paragraph
11 — Lining Up Paragraphs on the Left, Right, or in the Center
12 — Creating Lists
13 — Choosing (or Changing) the Style of a List
14 — Choosing a Font for Text
15 — Making Text Bigger or Smaller
16 — Making Text Bold, Italic, or Underlined
17 — Choosing the Color of Text

▶ **4: Making Links**

1 — Exploring How Links Work
2 — Choosing Where the Links in Your Personal Page Point
3 — Creating New Links from Scratch
4 — Linking Your Own Pages to Each Other to Make a Web Site
5 — Linking to a Particular Spot on a Page
6 — Linking to Files So Your Visitors Can Download Them
7 — Linking to Your Email So Visitors Can Contact You
8 — Checking That Links Go Where They're Supposed To

16 — Adding a Picture Background
17 — Finding and Adding Animations
18 — Finding Sound Clips
19 — Playing a Background Sound

Part ▶ **5: Adding Style to Your Pages**

1 — Choosing Text Colors and Background Colors
2 — Adding Lines to Divide Up a Page
3 — Changing the Look of a Line
4 — Finding Pictures
5 — Copying a Picture from the Web
6 — Creating Pictures
7 — Giving a Picture a Transparent Background
8 — Putting a Picture in a Page
9 — Changing the Size of a Picture
10 — Changing the Shape of a Picture
11 — Putting a Border Around a Picture
12 — Choosing a Picture's Alignment
13 — Controlling How Text Aligns to a Picture
14 — Using a Picture as a Link
15 — Creating a Times Square–Style Animated Marquee

Part ▶ **6: Creating Tables and Forms**

1 — Inserting a New Table
2 — Putting Text in Table Cells
3 — Putting Pictures in a Table
4 — Adding a Caption to a Table
5 — Dressing Up Tables with Borders
6 — Choosing Custom Border Colors
7 — Choosing a Background for a Table
8 — Creating an Interactive Form

Part ▶ **7: Publishing Your Page Online**

1 — Finding Space on a Web Server
2 — Learning More About the Server You've Chosen
3 — Getting Ready to Publish
4 — Running the Web Publishing Wizard
5 — Updating and Editing Your Page
6 — Viewing Your Page Through the Internet
7 — Getting Multiple Browser Programs for Testing
8 — Getting Your Own Domain

Part ▶ **8: Announcing Your Page**

1 — Finding Places to Promote Your Site
2 — Listing Your Page in the Yahoo! Directory
3 — Listing Your Page in the Excite Directory
4 — Checking Out the Site Submission Services
5 — Adding Your Web Address to Ads, Letterhead, and More
6 — Announcing Your Page by Email

Part ▶ **9: Super Editing: HTML**

1 — What Is HTML, Exactly?
2 — Creating a Web Page in HTML
3 — Adding a Picture Through HTML
4 — Applying Formatting to Text
5 — Learning How to Use All the HTML Tags

Part ▶ **10: Discovering Other Web Authoring Tools & Techniques**

1 — Finding Authoring Programs on the Web
2 — Learning About Microsoft FrontPage
3 — Learning About Netscape Composer
4 — Finding Graphics Utilities and Other Helpful Programs
5 — Downloading Programs from the Web
6 — Downloading WinZip
7 — Learning About Advanced Authoring Techniques

Executive Editor
Greg Wiegand

Acquisitions Editor
Angelina Ward

Development Editor
Gregory Harris

Managing Editor
Thomas F. Hayes

Project Editor
Leah Kirkpatrick

Copy Editor
Kay Hoskin

Indexer
Heather McNeill

Technical Editor
John Purdum

Proofreader
Jeanne Clark

Production
Cyndi Davis-Hubler

How to Use This Book

It's as Easy as 1-2-3

Each part of this book is made up of a series of short, instructional lessons, designed to help you understand basic information that you need to get the most out of your computer hardware and software.

 Click: Click the left mouse button once.

 Double-click: Click the left mouse button twice in rapid succession.

 Right-click: Click the right mouse button once.

 Pointer Arrow: Highlights an item on the screen you need to point to or focus on in the step or task.

 Selection: Highlights the area onscreen discussed in the step or task.

 Click & Type: Click once where indicated and begin typing to enter your text or data.

✓ Tips and ① Warnings give you a heads-up for any extra information you may need while working through the task.

② Each task includes a series of quick, easy steps designed to guide you through the procedure.

Drag

Drop

How to Drag: Point to the starting place or object. Hold down the mouse button (right or left per instructions), move the mouse to the new location, then release the button.

① Each step is fully illustrated to show you how it looks onscreen.

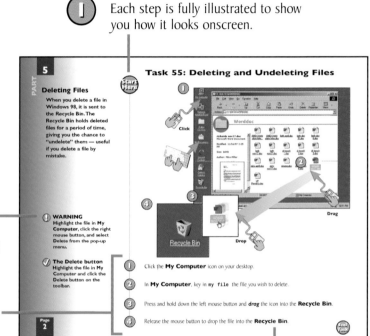

③ Items that you select or click in menus, dialog boxes, tabs, and windows are shown in **bold**. Information you type is in a `special font`.

 Next Step: If you see this symbol, it means the task you're working on continues on the next page.

 End Task: Task is complete.

Introduction to Web Page Publishing

It wasn't that long ago that the perception of a Webmaster was close to that of a god. Those also were the days when you had to know how to hand-code HTML to create Web pages. That meant launching a text editor of some kind and scribbling all kinds of arcane formatting codes. Thank goodness those days are over! Now anyone can develop a Web page—thanks to WYSIWYG (what you see is what you get) programs such as FrontPage Express and Netscape Composer. If you can use word-processing tools, such as Microsoft Word, you can create Web pages because much of the functionality is the same. Creating Web pages today is a breeze.

The tools you need to begin developing your own Web pages are your PC, Windows (Windows 95, 98, or NT), an Internet account, and your own creativity. The only other tool you need is the one you are reading right now.

In this book, you'll find not only clear, simple steps for creating Web pages and making them look great, but also instructions for getting a free Web page authoring tool. The tool and the steps work together to make you an aspiring Webmaster—the *Easy* way.

PART 1

Getting a Web Page Authoring Tool

Before we jump right in and start having fun, we must first check to see if you have a Web authoring tool. A Web authoring tool allows you to create a Web page in much the same way you create a document with a word processor. The better Web authoring tools, like the better word processors, are called **WYSIWYG** (what you see is what you get), because while you're working on a Web page, the tool shows you what the page will look like online.

Many popular WYSIWYG Web authoring tools are available. This book uses one of those tools, Microsoft's FrontPage Express, for three reasons: It's free, it's easy to get, and it's an excellent tool to begin learning about Web authoring. In this part of the book, you learn how to get FrontPage Express (or find out whether you already have it!), and get started using it.

Note that FrontPage Express has much in common with other WYSIWYG Web authoring tools, including its bigger brother, FrontPage. (FrontPage is Microsoft's pro-level Web tool, not to be confused with FrontPage Express.) The experience you gain here in FrontPage Express will move right along with you, if and when you choose to move up to another tool. If you have another simple Web editor, such as Netscape Composer, you'll find most of the steps to be fairly similar.

Tasks

Task #   Page #

1   Do You Already **Have** a Web-Authoring Tool?   4

2   Surfing to Microsoft's Web Site to Get an Authoring Tool   5

3   Downloading the Setup Program   6

4   Installing Internet Explorer and FrontPage Express   8

5   Opening FrontPage Express   10

6   Discovering FrontPage Express's Toolbars   11

There's a good chance you already have FrontPage Express and can skip Tasks 2, 3, and 4. FrontPage Express is a part of Microsoft Internet Explorer 4 and 5, is included free on many PCs, and is piggy-backed free in many other tools (especially Microsoft software) and products, such as Windows 98. So you may already have FrontPage Express. But, here's how to find out for sure.

✅ Installing Internet Explorer 5

On some computers (especially new ones), Internet Explorer 5 has not yet been installed. However, an icon for installing it should appear on the desktop. This icon, sometimes labeled Set Up Internet Explorer, starts the installation process. If you don't have FrontPage Express, but do see the Internet Explorer icon on your desktop, skip ahead to Task 4.

Task 1: Do You Already *Have* a Web-Authoring Tool?

Start Here

Click

Click

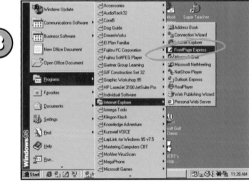

1 From your Windows taskbar, click the **Start** button.

2 Depending on the location chosen during installation, choose **Programs**, and then click **Internet Tools** or **Internet Explorer**.

3 If FrontPage Express appears in the Internet Tools or Internet Explorer menu, you can skip ahead to Task 5. If not, see Task 2.

End Task

Task 2: Surfing to Microsoft's Web Site to Get an Authoring Tool

Click

Open your Web browser (a previous version of Internet Explorer, Netscape Navigator, or whatever you usually use to surf the Web) and connect to the Internet.

Go to Microsoft's Internet Explorer Web site at `www.microsoft.com/ie/default.htm`.

If you don't already have FrontPage Express, you can get it (free, of course) simply by installing Internet Explorer 5 and selecting the right options. It's also included with many Microsoft tools. The following task shows you how to get it from the Internet.

 Getting IE5 on CD-ROM

On the Internet Explorer Web site, you'll find not only a link for getting Internet Explorer online, but also a link for ordering Internet Explorer on CD for a small fee ($6.95 + tax, at this writing). Internet Explorer is a very large program, so it may take an hour or more to download from the Internet, depending on your modem speed. If you don't like tying up your phone line, you can order it on **CD**. In addition, you might want to check out the **System Requirements** link from the site menu on the left of the page to review what you need to download and run Internet Explorer.

Task 3: Downloading the Setup Program

Getting Internet Explorer and FrontPage Express from the Web happens in two parts. The first is getting the setup program ie5setup.exe, as described here. The second is using that program to complete the download and setup, as described in Task 4.

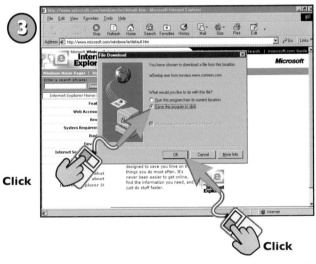

Click

Click

Click

(✓) **Be Prepared for a Delay**
The Saving dialog box displays a time estimate to let you know approximately how long it will take to download the setup file. So, now would be a good time to catch up on that reading (like this book!), take a nap, or do whatever your heart desires.

① Go to Microsoft's Internet Explorer Web site (**www.microsoft.com/ie/default.htm**) as described in Task 2.

② Click the **Download Now** button.

③ Select **Save This Program to Disk** and then click **OK**.

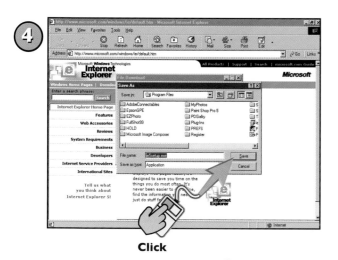

Click

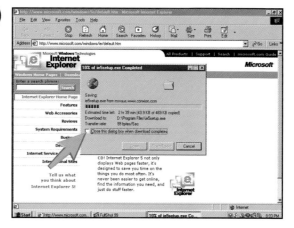

④ Choose a folder (or your desktop) to save the Internet Explorer setup program in, and click **Save** to begin downloading the ie5setup.exe file.

⑤ Upon completion, the Saving dialog box disappears if the **Close This Dialog Box When Download Completes** check box is checked.

The Internet Explorer setup program sets up Internet Explorer (and FrontPage Express) on your PC. If you downloaded the setup program (as in Task 3), then the program automatically downloads the rest of Internet Explorer from the Web; if you have the setup program on CD, then it automatically copies the Internet Explorer files from the CD.

I recommend that you have all programs closed before installing Internet Explorer, because you will be required to restart your computer after the installation completes. Now on with the show.

✓ **Your Browser Doesn't Matter**

Again, you do not have to use Internet Explorer for surfing the Web in order to use FrontPage Express. You can continue to use whatever you usually use for Web surfing, and use FrontPage Express for Web authoring jobs.

Task 4: Installing Internet Explorer and FrontPage Express

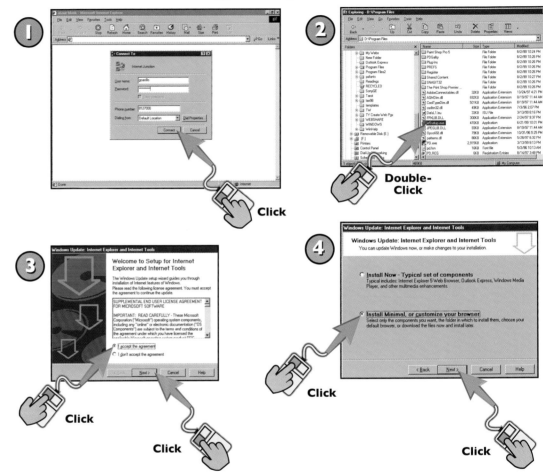

Start Here

Click

Double-Click

Click

Click

Click

Click

① Connect to the Internet (or insert the CD, if you have Internet Explorer 5 on CD).

② Locate the file folder to which you downloaded the setup program and double-click the **ie5setup.exe** file icon.

③ Select **I Accept the Agreement** and click **Next**.

④ Select the **Install Minimal, or Customize Your Browser** option and click **Next**.

Next Step

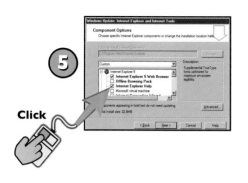

Click

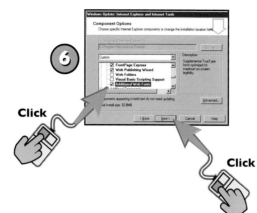

Click

Click

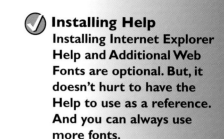

✅ **Installing Help**
Installing Internet Explorer Help and Additional Web Fonts are optional. But, it doesn't hurt to have the Help to use as a reference. And you can always use more fonts.

Click

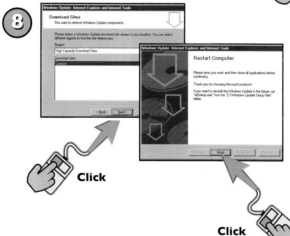

Click

Click

✅ **Performing a Custom Installation**
With previous versions of Internet Explorer, you would select a typical install to install both the browser and FrontPage Express. However, with Internet Explorer 5, FrontPage Express is only installed if you choose to install it. So, doing a custom install saves you the extra step of having to perform two installations— one for the browser and one for FrontPage Express.

5️⃣ Make sure you check the following selections: **Internet Explorer 5 Web Browser**, **Internet Explorer Help**…

6️⃣ …**FrontPage Express**, **Web Publishing Wizard**, and **Additional Web Fonts**. Click **Next**.

7️⃣ Click **Yes** to continue.

8️⃣ Accept the default download site by clicking **Next**. Click **Finish** to restart your computer.

✅ **Choosing Other Installation Options**
The other options you can install are up to you. They are not required to perform the tasks in this book. However, you may want to play with them later. So, it's up to you.

Task 5: Opening FrontPage Express

After Internet Explorer and FrontPage Express have been installed, you are ready to start creating Web pages. Here's how to open FrontPage Express and get ready to work.

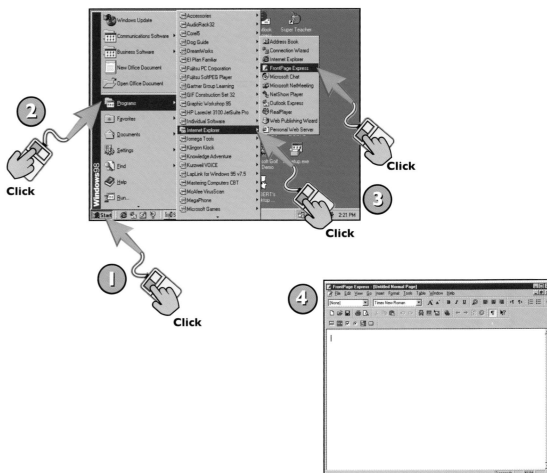

(✓) **Opening a Blank Document**
When FrontPage Express opens, it automatically opens a new, blank Web page file. You can start typing right away to begin creating your first Web page—although in Part 2, "Building Your First Web Page," you'll discover even easier ways to get a new page going.

1. From your Windows taskbar, click the **Start** button.

2. Click **Programs**.

3. Click **Accessories** or, depending on the locations chosen during installation, **Internet Explorer**, and then click **Internet Tools**. Click **FrontPage Express**.

4. FrontPage Express opens.

End Task

Task 6: Discovering FrontPage Express's Toolbars

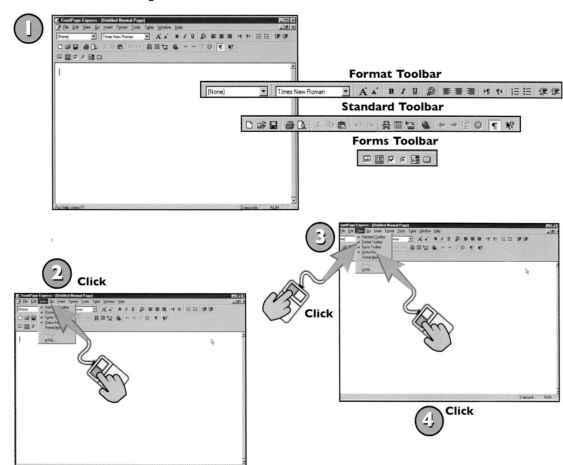

Format Toolbar

Standard Toolbar

Forms Toolbar

You perform many functions in FrontPage Express by clicking buttons on three toolbars: Standard, Format, and Forms. The toolbars appear as three rows of buttons near the top of the FrontPage Express window, and each can be displayed (for ready use) or hidden (to free up more screen area for examining your creations.)

✓ **Getting Information from ToolTips**
Every button (or list box) on the toolbars has a "ToolTip," a name that appears to identify the button. To learn the name of any button or list box, point to it (don't click) and pause a moment without moving the mouse.

✓ **Scanning the ToolTip List**
To quickly see the names of all the buttons in one toolbar, point to the button or list box that's farthest to the left, but don't click. Move your mouse to the right and as you pass each button, its name displays.

② Click

③ Click

④ Click

① Open FrontPage Express and look at the three rows of buttons beneath the menu bar.

② Click **View**. On the menu, a check mark appears next to the name of each toolbar that is currently displayed.

③ To hide a toolbar, click its name.

④ To re-display a toolbar you've hidden, click **View** and click the toolbar's name again.

End Task

Building Your First Web Page

So you're probably staring at a blank page thinking about how you should begin. That's where FrontPage Express can really help. When you create your first Web pages, it helps to have a head start—a basic prefab page or template you can mold to your own liking.

That's what FrontPage Express's Personal Home Page Wizard provides—a head start. It doesn't give you a finished page all by itself; you still need to go in and personalize the page that the wizard produces. But you'll find that creating your first page is easier when you don't start out with a blank page. The tasks in this part show you how to use the wizard to crank out that first page in a flash.

Of course, you may soon want to create a new, blank Web page you can fill with your own ideas from scratch. By the end of this chapter, you'll know how to do that, too.

Tasks

Task #		Page #
1	Starting the Personal Home Page Wizard	14
2	Choosing What to Include on the Page	15
3	Naming the Page and Its File	16
4	Choosing the Style for Your List of Links	17
5	Choosing the Information About You to Include	18
6	Putting Contact Information at the Bottom of Your Page	19
7	Choosing How to Receive Feedback from Your Visitors	20
8	Choosing the Order of Information on Your Page	21
9	Producing the Web Page	22
10	Saving the New Page	23
11	Closing and Re-Opening a Page File	24
12	Opening a Web Page You Haven't Used Lately	25
13	Changing Your Web Page Title	26
14	Starting a Completely Blank Page	27
15	Checking Out Your New Page in a Web Browser	28

We begin your trip through the Personal Home Page Wizard by starting a new page in FrontPage Express. So, here we go.

Task 1: Starting the Personal Home Page Wizard

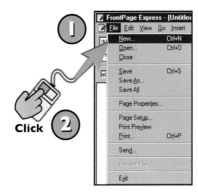

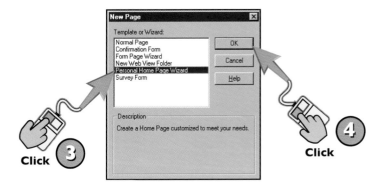

1. Open FrontPage Express.

2. Click **File**, and then select **New**.

3. Click **Personal Home Page Wizard**.

4. Click **OK**.

Task 2: Choosing What to Include on the Page

The Personal Home Page Wizard provides several different options from which to choose. Each option is used to display different types of information on the Web page. You choose which sections you want on your Web page.

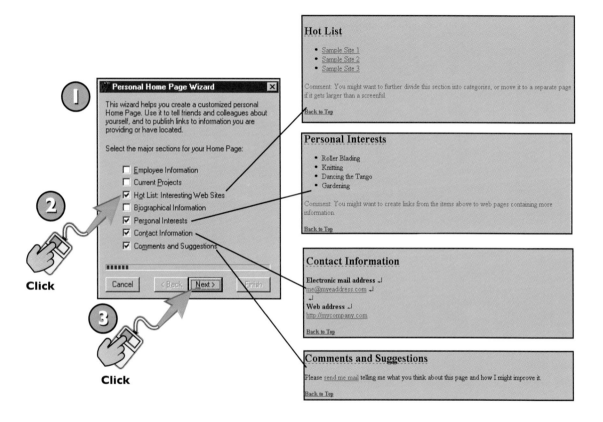

Click

Click

(1) Review the list of items, and decide what information you want to include on your Web page.

(2) For practice, leave check marks only next to **Hot List**, **Personal Interests**, **Contact Information**, and **Comments and Suggestions**.

(3) Click **Next**.

 Checking a Check Box
To add a check mark to an empty check box, point to the box and click. To remove a check mark from a check box, point to the checked box and click.

Task 3: Naming the Page and Its File

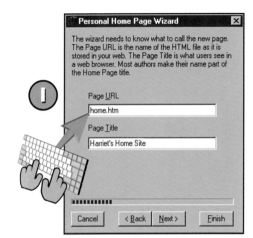

To save and use your Web page, you must give it a filename. You should give your Web page files short, simple filenames, always ending in **.htm** or **.html**. Usually, the first Web page you create is considered the "home" page. So, a lot of people call their first Web page just that, home.html. The home page is the place from which all links originate. (You'll learn more about links in Part 4, "Making Links.") In addition to a filename, all Web pages also have a title, which identifies the page contents to visitors.

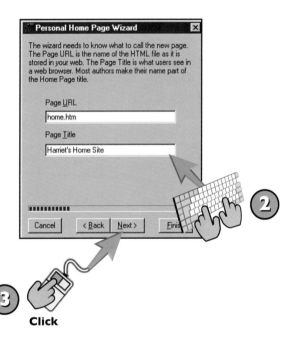

Click

Changing Previous Decisions in a Wizard
At any point while working with the wizard, you can click **Back** to move backward to earlier tasks and change the choices you made. Your choices don't become final until you click **Finish**.

 In the **Page URL** box, type a simple filename for your Web page file and end the name with **.htm** or **.html**.

 In the **Page Title** box, type a descriptive title for your page.

 Click **Next**.

Task 4: Choosing the Style for Your List of Links

Start Here

The wizard can whip up a snazzy list of links—a "Hot List"—so that your visitors can jump straight from your page to other pages you want to share with them. Actually, the links are "dummy" links—links that don't go anywhere—until you tell them where to go, as you learn to do in **Part 4.** The wizard just helps you get started.

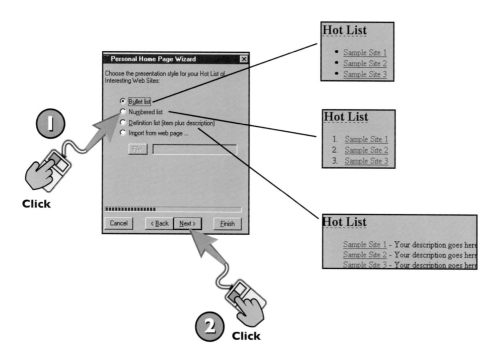

Click

2 **Click**

1 Click the name of the style you want formatted for the links in your Hot List.

2 Click **Next**.

Importing Links
When you have more experience creating Web pages, you may choose the fourth item, **Import from Web Page.** This item copies a list of links from another page.

Task 5: Choosing the Information About You to Include

Start Here

The Personal Home Page Wizard can include a variety of different sections, listing information about you. You choose which sections to include.

✓ **Differentiating List Types**
Bullet list style lists each of the items in your list as a "bullet" character, Numbered list numbers each item from one up, and Definition list indents your list and creates extra space following each item for a description, which you can type later.

✓ **The Wizard Isn't the Final Word**
When you're done with the wizard, you can edit, expand, or enhance your page any way you like. So don't worry too much about the choices you make at this point.

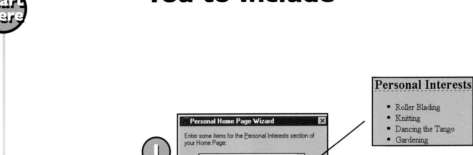

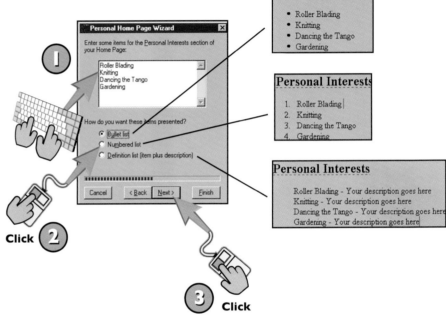

Click ②

③ Click

① Type a list of personal interests in the white box, and press **Enter** after every entry. You can enter as many items as you like.

② Choose how you want the list displayed by selecting one of the option buttons: **Bullet List**, **Numbered List**, or **Definition List**.

③ Click **Next**.

End Task

Task 6: Putting Contact Information at the Bottom of Your Page

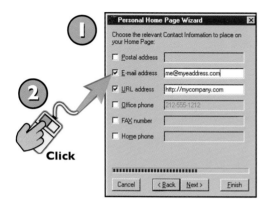

Click

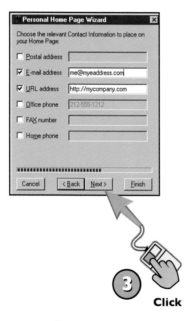

Click

Often, a Web page is intended to provide not one-way communication, but a two-way dialogue. You have something to tell your visitors, but you also want to hear back from them—feedback. That's where adding contact information comes in.

✓ **Checking Check Boxes**
To add a check mark to an empty check box, point to the box and click. To remove a check mark from a check box, point to the box and click.

✓ **Keeping Your Private Information Private!**
On a business Web page, it's often appropriate to include a postal address and a telephone number. But for privacy's sake, never put your home phone number or mailing address on a Web page. Anyone who wants to contact you may do so by email.

1 Review the list of check boxes and decide what Contact Information you want to use so that your visitors can contact you.

2 Change the check boxes so that check marks appear only next to items you want to include. For practice, let's just select **E-mail Address** and **URL Address**.

3 Click **Next**.

End Task

Task 7: Choosing How to Receive Feedback from Your Visitors

Start Here

As the last selection, you now need to decide how you would like feedback sent to you from your visitors. You can use forms, which the visitor fills out, and their comments are either stored in a Web page or in a data file. You can then review their comments later. Or, you can choose to have comments emailed to you directly.

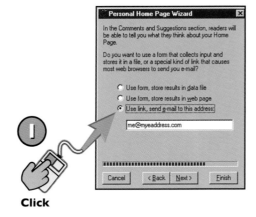

①

Click

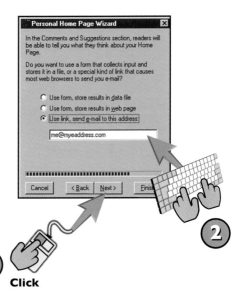

②

③ Click

① Select the method of feedback. For the purposes of this task, choose **Use link, Send E-mail to This Address**.

② Enter your email address in the text box.

③ Click **Next**.

End Task

Task 8: Choosing the Order of Information on Your Page

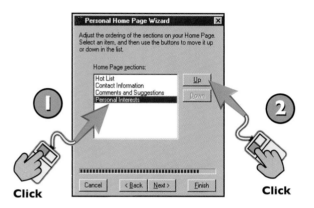

Click

Click

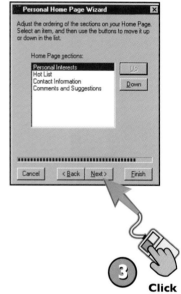

We're almost there, but first you must decide what order you want for each of the sections you created previously to be listed on your Web page.

③ **Click**

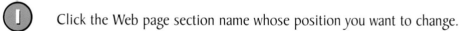

① Click the Web page section name whose position you want to change.

② To move the item higher on the page, click **Up**. To move the item lower on the page, click **Down**.

③ When the sections are in the order you want, click **Next**.

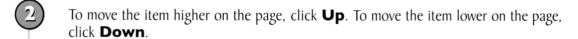

Task 9: Producing the Web Page

After making all your choices, you now must tell the wizard to put the selections together and show them to you.

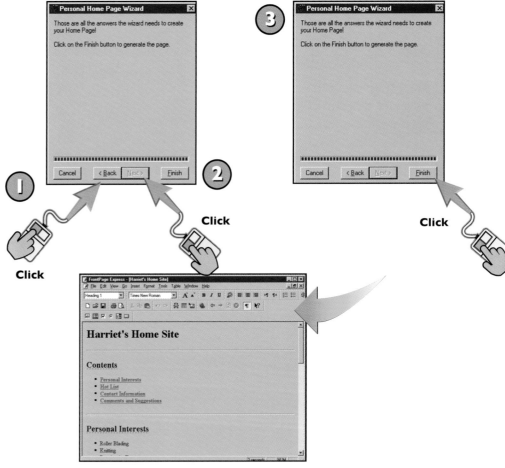

(1) If you want to review your choices, click **Back**.

(2) Make any changes you want, then click **Next** until you return to the final dialog box.

(3) Click **Finish**. The page appears in FrontPage Express, where you can make additional changes and test it.

Task 10: Saving the New Page

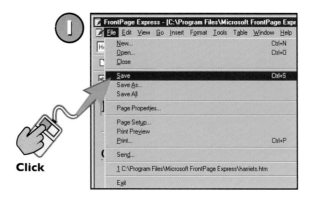

Click

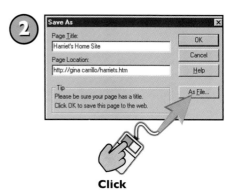

Click

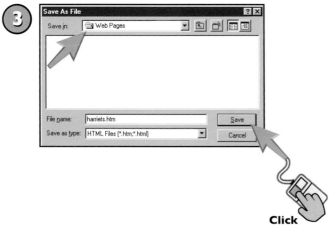

Click

If you have any experience in other creative programs—such as word processors—you know how important it is to save your files. Web page files are no different. You should save your Web page right after creating it, and then again anytime you make changes to it.

✓ Saving to Specific Folders

To save the file in a specific folder (for example, Web Pages, as used in previous examples), click the drop-down arrow next to the **Save In** box, at the top of the Save As File dialog box. Locate the **Web Pages** (or whatever you called yours) folder and click it. Then click **Save**.

① Click **File**, and then choose **Save**.

② Click **As File**.

③ Choose a folder to save the Web file in and click **Save**.

✓ Saving Again Is Even Easier

After the first time you save a file, you'll no longer need to perform steps 2 and 3 when you save again. Simply performing step 1 saves the file.

Task 11: Closing and Re-Opening a Page File

As you create your Web pages, you'll probably end up making changes as you go along. So, you'll need to open existing files, and then save and close them when you're done.

 Start Here

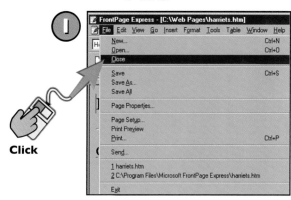

Click

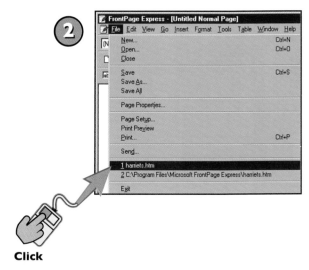

Click

 FrontPage Prompts You to Save

If you did not save your changes before telling FrontPage Express to close the file, a message displays asking if you want to save your changes. Click **Yes**. FrontPage saves your file and then closes it. So you don't have to worry about exiting the program and losing changes.

1 To close a Web page (without closing FrontPage Express), click **File** and choose **Close**.

2 To open a Web page you've used recently, click **File**, and then choose the filename from the bottom of the File menu.

 End Task

Task 12: Opening a Web Page You Haven't Used Lately

Start Here

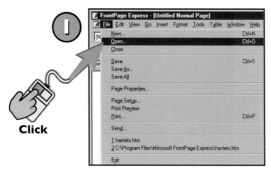

Click

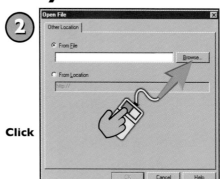

Click

If a file you want to edit is not among the files you've worked with recently, its name won't appear on the File menu. In that case, here's how to open any Web page file on your PC.

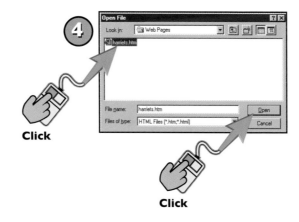

Click

Click

Click

① Click **File** and choose **Open**.

② Click **Browse**.

③ Use the **Look In** list to navigate to the folder where you stored the Web page.

④ From the Open File dialog box, choose the filename and click **Open**.

End Task

Task 13: Changing Your Web Page Title

The real "title" of your Web page does not appear within the layout of the page itself. It appears in the title bar of the browser through which the page is viewed, although Web authors often duplicate the title as a big bold heading at the top of the page. The title is important because it identifies your page in search tools like Yahoo! and in visitor bookmark lists.

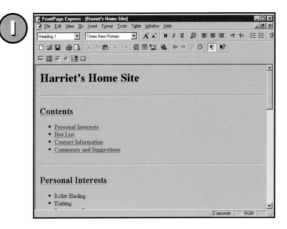

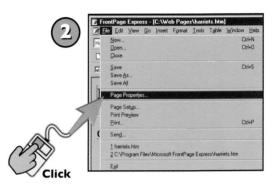

Click

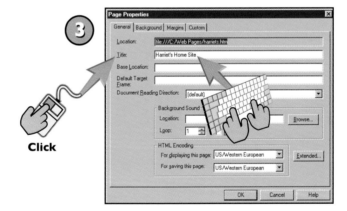

Click

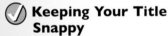

Keeping Your Title Snappy

Make your title short, but clear and descriptive. In the example, it's clear that this is a personal home page for someone named Harriet. There are probably few sites with that name, but you never know. So, choose your title wisely.

 Open the Web page in FrontPage Express.

 Click **File** and choose **Page Properties**.

 Click in the **Title** box on the **General** tab and change the title.

End Task

Task 14: Starting a Completely Blank Page

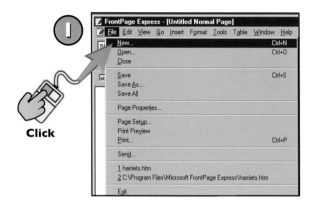

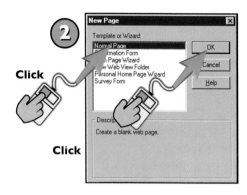

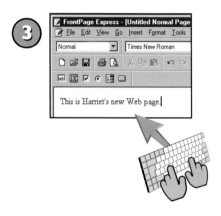

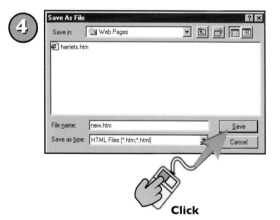

Now that you know how to create a basic page using the wizard, it's time to learn how to start one from scratch. It really doesn't matter which way you start—what matters is that you know about both methods, so you can choose the one you need.

Click

Click

Click

Click

Click

① Click **File** and choose **New**.

② Click **Normal Page** and then click **OK**.

③ Start typing and formatting the contents of the page, as you learn to do in upcoming parts of this book.

④ Save your Web page early and often.

✓ **Form Options**
Some of the other choices on the New dialog box—Confirmation Form, Form Page Wizard, and Survey Form—all help you add interactive *forms* to your Web site that your visitors can use to answer questions or provide feedback. (See Part 6, "Creating Tables and Forms," for more information about forms.)

Task 15: Checking Out Your New Page in a Web Browser

Now we're ready to see the results of your first masterpiece in a browser. In FrontPage Express, your Web pages will appear pretty much the same as they do when viewed through a browser. However, it's a good idea to preview your page through your Web browser from time to time to evaluate its appearance.

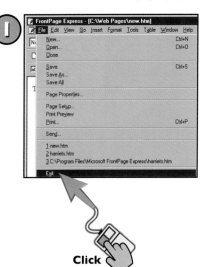

Click

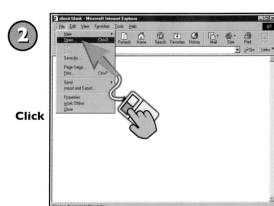

Click

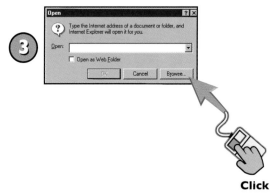

Click

Click

Start Here

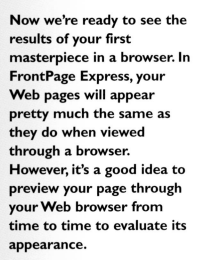

✓ Locating Your File
Task 10 suggested saving your Web page files in the Web Pages folder, so you may find the Web file there.

1 In FrontPage Express, click **File** and choose **Exit**.

2 Open your browser without connecting to the Internet, click **File**, and then select **Open**.

3 Click **Browse**.

Next Step

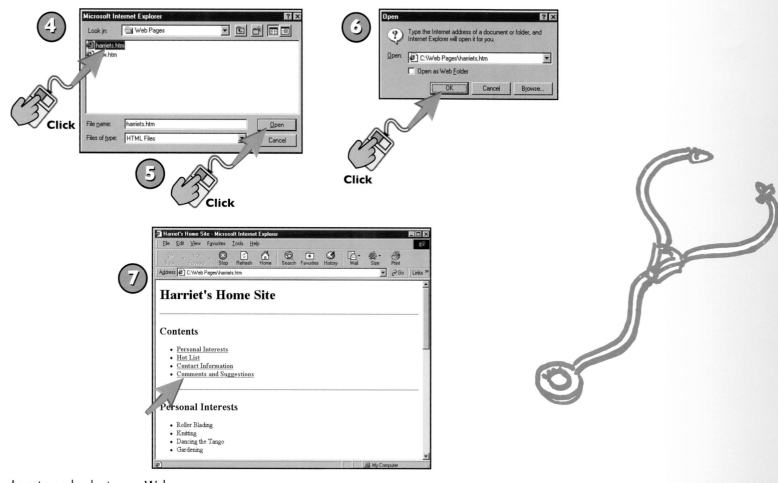

4 Locate and select your Web page.

5 Click **Open**.

6 Click **OK**.

7 Voila! There's your Web page. You can now click the links to test them.

Making Your Page Say What You Want

The main purpose of creating a Web page is to share information with your viewers. And to do that, you need to make the information understandable, right? That means using text to share that information. Yes, you will use pictures or other objects as well, but the efficient use of text is the key to making your Web page say what you want.

In this part, you explore the ways you create, edit, and format Web page text in a Web authoring program. You'll find that the job is very much like using a word processor.

Tasks

Task #		Page #
1	Selecting Text	32
2	Changing Text on a Page	33
3	Typing New Text	34
4	Typing Symbols and Special Characters	35
5	Deleting Text	36
6	Fixing Mistakes	37
7	Copying Text	38
8	Moving Text	39
9	Choosing the Style of a Paragraph	40
10	Indenting a Paragraph	41
11	Lining Up Paragraphs on the Left, Right, or in the Center	42
12	Creating Lists	43
13	Choosing (or Changing) the Style of a List	44
14	Choosing a Font for Text	45
15	Making Text Bigger or Smaller	46
16	Making Text Bold, Italic, or Underlined	47
17	Choosing the Color of Text	48

To perform most activities involving text, such as changing the style of text or replacing text with different text, you must first select, or *highlight*, the text you want to work with. You select text in FrontPage Express in the same way you select text in most other word-processing programs.

✓ Understanding Formatting Types

There are two basic kinds of formatting: paragraph formatting (changing the appearance of whole paragraphs) and character formatting (changing the appearance only of selected characters). When applying character formatting, you must select precisely the characters you want to format. But when applying paragraph formatting, you need only select part of the paragraph. If any part of it is highlighted, any paragraph formatting you apply affects the whole paragraph.

Task 1: Selecting Text

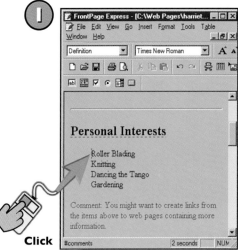

Click

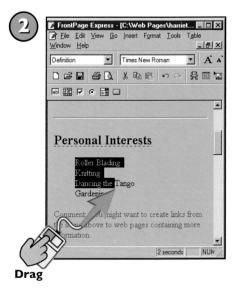

Drag

① For practice, open the Web page you created in Part 2 and point to the beginning of the text that you want to select.

② Click and drag to highlight the selection: Drag to the right to select all or part of a line; drag down to select multiple lines.

Task 2: Changing Text on a Page

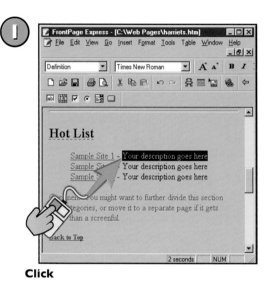

Click

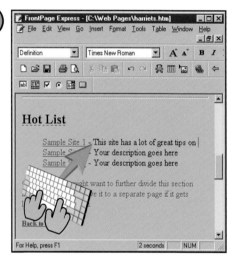

If you used the Personal Home Page Wizard to build your first Web page, you have a lot of sample text in your page that you need to replace with text of your own. Even if you did not use the wizard, replacing text is an essential editing skill.

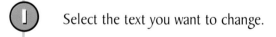

① Select the text you want to change.

② Type your new text.

 Overwriting Existing Text
Anything you type automatically replaces the selected text. The new text usually picks up the formatting of the text you are replacing.

Task 3: Typing New Text

In addition to replacing text, you'll need to add new text.

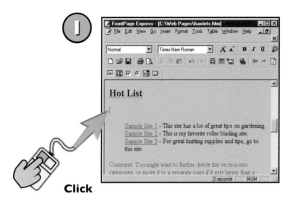

Click

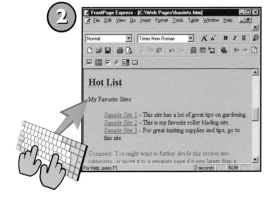

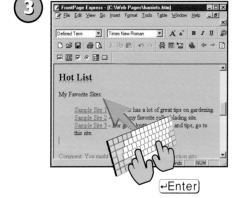

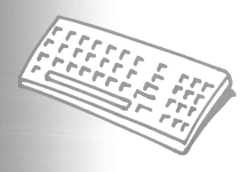

✅ **Saving Early, Saving Often**

Don't forget to save your Web page file often, especially after adding or changing text.

1. Point to the spot on the page where you want to add new text, and click. The **_edit cursor_**, a flashing vertical bar, appears where you clicked.

2. Type your text. When you reach the end of a line, just keep typing; the edit cursor jumps automatically to the beginning of the next line.

3. To end a paragraph and start a new one, press **Enter**.

Task 4: Typing Symbols and Special Characters

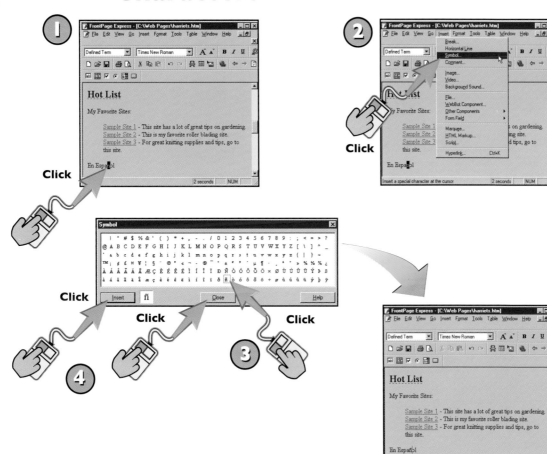

There will be times when you need characters that don't appear on your keyboard, such as the copyright symbol or accented characters used in other languages. For such occasions, FrontPage Express offers its Symbol menu.

1. Point to the spot in the text where you want to insert the character and click to position the edit cursor there.

2. Click **Insert**, then choose **Symbol**.

3. Click the symbol you want to insert. After you click it, it appears next to the **Insert** button.

4. Click **Insert** to insert the character. Click **Close**.

✓ **Reviewing Your Symbols After Font Changes**
If you change the font (as you learn to do in Task 14) of text containing symbols, check the symbols carefully, and re-apply them if necessary. Sometimes changing fonts changes the way symbols appear.

Task 5: Deleting Text

OK, so you did a brain
dump and now need to do a
little tweaking. Not a
problem. You can remove
text and start again, if
needed.

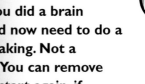

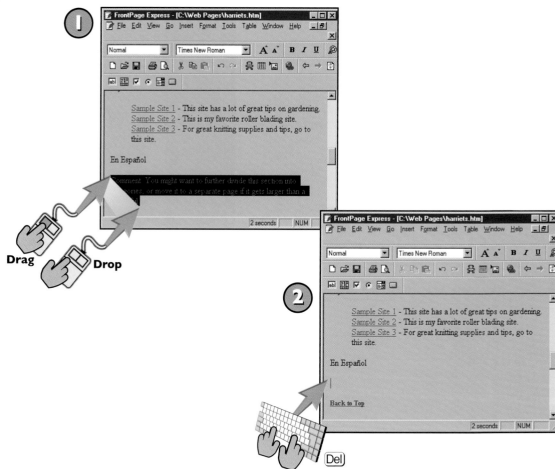

1. Select the text you want to delete.

2. Press the **Delete** key.

Task 6: Fixing Mistakes

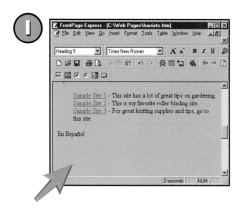

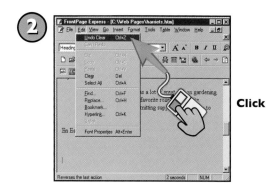

Click

Oops! Maybe you deleted something you didn't mean to in Task 5. If you delete text and then suddenly realize that you want it back, you can use the steps in this task to recover the deleted text. The catch, however, is that you must perform these steps immediately after the mistake; if you perform another action in the meantime, you'll undo *that* action instead of undoing the earlier mistake.

 Undoing Several Actions

If you make several changes that you end up not wanting, you can't use undo to fix them. However, you can reverse those mistakes by closing the file without saving it (click **File**, then choose **Close**). The only problem with this method is that you undo not only the mistakes, but *everything* you did to the page since the last time you saved it, possibly including some good stuff you'll then have to redo.

1 Perform any action in FrontPage Express, such as deleting some text.

2 Click **Edit**, then choose **Undo Clear**.

3 Deleted text reappears. If you change your mind again, and want to **undo** the undo (putting the page back the way it was right after Step 1), click **Edit** and choose **Redo Clear**.

Task 7: Copying Text

If you have a block of text you want to use in more than one place on your page, there is no need to type it over and over. You can simply type it once and then copy it wherever you need it.

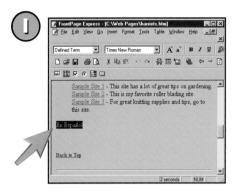

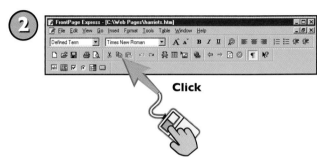

Click

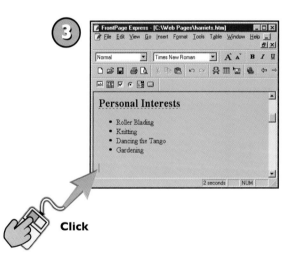

Click

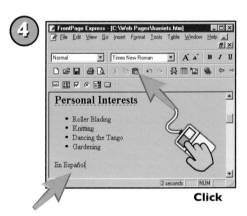

Click

✓ **Repeating a Copy Operation**

After step 4, you can move ahead to other editing activities, or you can copy the same text you selected in step 1 again—and as many more times as you want—by repeating steps 3 and 4 for each copy you want to make.

Select the text you want to copy.

Click the **Copy** button on the Standard toolbar.

Point to the spot where you want to copy the text and click to position the edit cursor there.

Click the **Paste** button on the Standard toolbar. The text appears.

End Task

Task 8: Moving Text

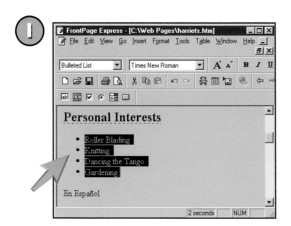

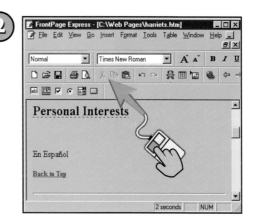

Click

Moving text is really just like copying—except that you don't leave the original text behind. You *cut* it from one place, then *copy* it in another.

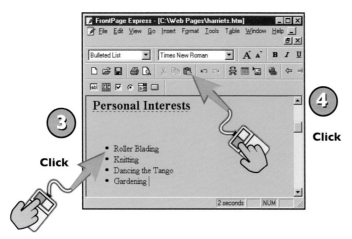

Click

Click

① Select the text you want to move.

② Click the **Cut** button on the Standard toolbar.

③ Point to the spot where you want to move the text, and click to position the edit cursor there.

④ Click the **Paste** button on the Standard toolbar. The text appears.

✓ Repeating a Paste Operation

Just like copying, after moving text you can paste as many copies as you want of the text you cut in step 2. Just repeat steps 3 and 4 for each copy you need.

End Task

The most important part of controlling the appearance of text is choosing the text's **paragraph style** from the Change Style list. There are many styles, but the most important are the six **Heading styles** (Heading 1 is the largest, Heading 6 is the smallest), **Normal style** (used for ordinary paragraphs), and the **List styles** (which you'll meet in Task 12).

✓ **Formatting Paragraphs with Styles**
Paragraph styles are an example of paragraph formatting (not character formatting), so you do not need to highlight the whole paragraph. Select any part of the paragraph, or just put the edit cursor anywhere within the paragraph, and the style you choose will be applied to the entire paragraph.

✓ **Applying Styles to Several Paragraphs**
To apply a style to multiple, consecutive paragraphs at the same time, click anywhere in the first paragraph and drag down to the last paragraph. Then choose your style.

Task 9: Choosing the Style of a Paragraph

Click

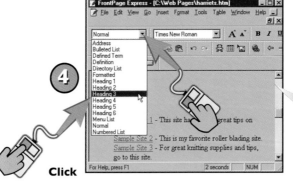

Click

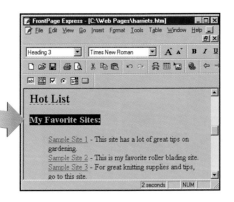

① Select the paragraph for which you want to change the style.

② Locate the **Change Style** list box at the left end of the Formatting toolbar. (Notice that it shows the style currently applied to the selected paragraph.)

③ Click the arrow on the right side of the list box to open the list.

④ Click the name of the style you want to apply.

Task 10: Indenting a Paragraph

Start Here

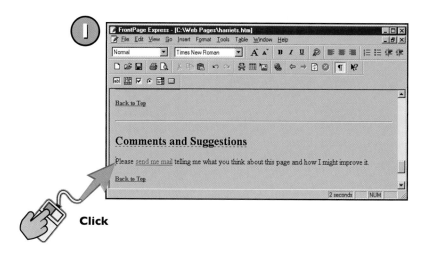

Click

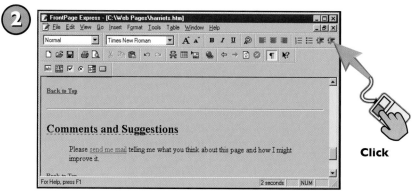

Click

To *indent* is to push text inward from the margin, in order to make it stand out on the page and to better show that the indented text is a part of the heading or other text above it. Indenting selected paragraphs can give your Web page structure and uniformity.

①　Place your cursor on the first line of a single paragraph or select multiple paragraphs that you want to indent.

②　Click the **Increase Indent** button on the Formatting toolbar.

✅ **Increasing the Indent**
To indent farther, click the **Increase Indent** button multiple times.

✅ **Decreasing the Indent**
To remove the indent, click the **Decrease Indent** button on the Formatting toolbar.

End Task

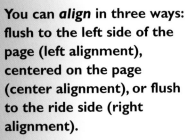

You can *align* in three ways: flush to the left side of the page (left alignment), centered on the page (center alignment), or flush to the ride side (right alignment).

Task 11: Lining Up Paragraphs on the Left, Right, or in the Center

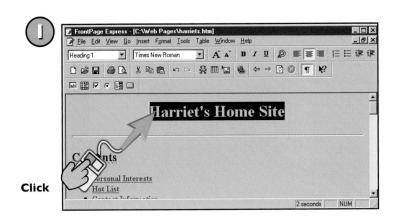

Click

 **Choosing Paragraph Alignment**

Most of the time, left alignment is best, especially for Normal-style paragraphs. Center can be nice for large headings (such as Heading 1 or Heading 2 style), especially if not used too much. Save right alignment for special needs.

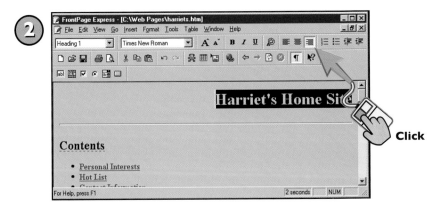

Click

Select the paragraph or paragraphs you want to align.

Click one of the three alignment buttons on the Formatting toolbar: **Align Left**, **Center**, or **Align Right**.

Task 12: Creating Lists

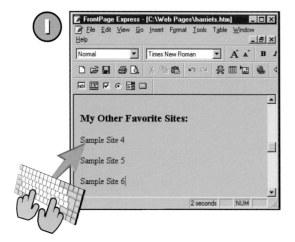

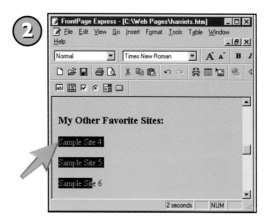

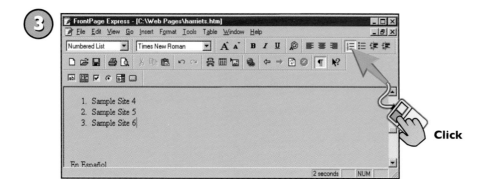

Click

There are two types of ordered lists: numbered and bulleted. (You can also create an unordered list, but it's far less interesting.) In a **numbered list**, the list items are preceded by consecutive numbers. In a **bulleted list**, each item in the list is preceded by a symbol, a bullet character. Lists are a great way to organize and present content in an easy-to-read fashion.

✅ **Formatting Lists**
List formatting is paragraph formatting, so you can select a list by starting the selection anywhere in the first item, then dragging down to anywhere in the last item.

✅ **Choosing a List Type**
When the order of the items in the list is important, as in step-by-step instructions, use a numbered list. When the order doesn't matter, use a bulleted list.

1 Type the list items, pressing **Enter** after each so that each list item is on a separate line.

2 Select the entire list.

3 Click one of the two list buttons on the Formatting toolbar: **Numbered List** or **Bulleted List**.

Creating a list involves just a click of a button. But, you don't have to settle for what you get. You can easily modify the appearance of a list, choose a different numbering style (A B C, I II III, and so on), or select a different bullet style.

Task 13: Choosing (or Changing) the Style of a List

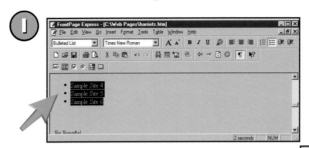

Start Here

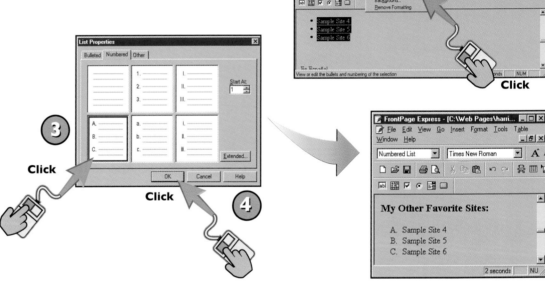

Click

Click

Click

Select the list.

Click **Format**, then choose **Bullets and Numbering**.

Click the new style you want to use from the options shown.

Click **OK**. The list appears in the new style.

Task 14: Choosing a Font for Text

Click

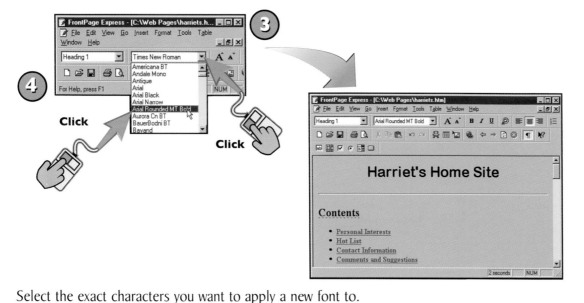

Click

Click

Click

The best way to control the style of text is to choose the appropriate paragraph style, as you did in Task 9. But beyond the styles, you can dress up text even more by choosing a different font.

✓ Applying Fonts

Fonts are a form of character formatting, not paragraph formatting, so they affect only the exact characters you select. In order to apply a font to a whole paragraph, you must select the whole paragraph. The same is true of the character formatting you discover in Tasks 15, 16, and 17.

✓ Choosing Common Fonts

Some browsers don't support various, nonstandard fonts. If you use nonstandard fonts, the browsers still see your text, but they won't see it in its original style. Some standard fonts like **Arial** and **Times New Roman** are usually safe.

1. Select the exact characters you want to apply a new font to.

2. Locate the **Change Font** list box in the Formatting toolbar. Notice that the box tells the name of the font that's now used for the selected text.

3. Click the arrow on the right side of the list box to open the list.

4. Click the name of the font you want to apply. The text appears in the new font.

Task 15: Making Text Bigger or Smaller

The paragraph style determines size. For example, if text set in Heading 3 style looks too small to you, the best solution is to change it to a bigger style, such as Heading 2 or Heading 1. However, you can fine-tune the size of selected text easily when the size chosen by the style isn't exactly what you want.

✓ **Changing Text Size by Larger Increments**
You can click the **Increase Text Size** or **Decrease Text Size** buttons multiple times to make text bigger or smaller. For example, to make text two levels bigger, click the **Increase Text Size** button twice.

✓ **Text Size Has Limits**
If you click **Increase Text Size** and the selected text does not get any bigger, the text is already set at the largest size allowed. Similarly, if **Decrease Text Size** does nothing, the text is already set at the minimum size allowed.

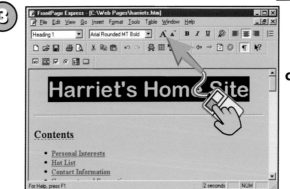

Click

Click

Click

1. Select the exact characters you want to make bigger or smaller.

2. Locate the two buttons to the right of the Change Font list on the Formatting toolbar.

3. To make the selected text larger, click the **Increase Text Size** button. To make the selected text smaller, click the **Decrease Text Size** button.

Task 16: Making Text Bold, Italic, or Underlined

Start Here

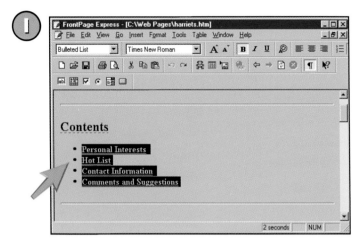

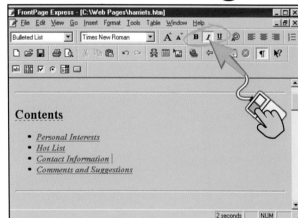

Click

Text and paragraph formatting, and the fonts you use are all important. However, **bold**, *italic* and <u>underlining</u> are valuable tools also. They are great for emphasis or for making text match editorial standards (such as setting book titles in italics). Though valuable tools, use them sparingly—overuse can make text busy and hard to read.

✓ **Removing Formatting**
To remove bold, italic, or underlining, select the text and click the button again. For example, to remove bolded formatting, select it and click the **Bold** button.

✓ **Combining Formatting Types**
You can combine these kinds of formatting; for example, you can make the selected text both bold and italic by clicking the **Bold** button, then the **Italic** button.

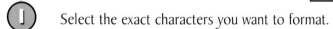

1 Select the exact characters you want to format.

2 Locate the group of three buttons to the right of the Decrease Text Size button on the Formatting toolbar.

3 Click the **Bold**, **Italic**, or **Underline** buttons to format the selected characters.

End Task

Task 17: Choosing the Color of Text

In Part 5, you learn how to choose a coordinated color scheme for your Web page—a scheme for making sure that all the colors used for text, background, and other objects all work together. If you do that, you probably won't choose colors selectively for blocks of text. Still, you might want to give a heading or other selected text unique color.

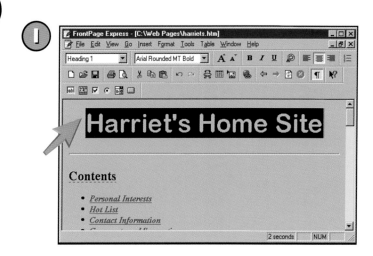

Click

Creating Custom Text Colors

If none of the colors that appear in the Color dialog box appeal to you, click the **Define Custom Colors** button. A palette displays, showing all the colors that are possible on your PC, as it is currently configured. Click the palette to create a Custom color, then apply that color by clicking the square in which it appears.

Select the exact characters you want to choose a color for.

Click the **Text Color** button on the Formatting toolbar.

Next Step

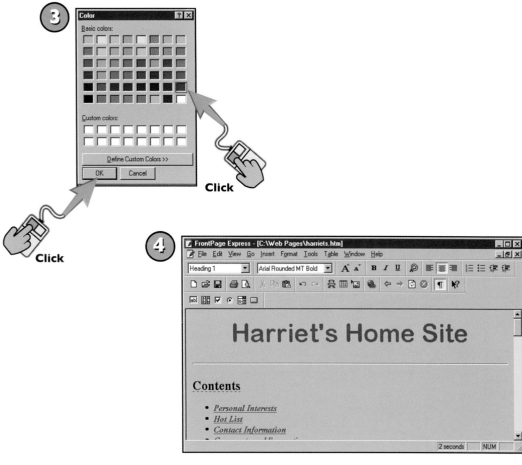

Click

Click

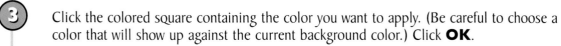

③ Click the colored square containing the color you want to apply. (Be careful to choose a color that will show up against the current background color.) Click **OK**.

④ The text appears in the new color.

4

Making Links

Links are the lifelines of the Web. They can be used to connect visitors to other areas on a single Web page or to separate pages. They also do other stuff, such as begin to download files. Without links, the Web wouldn't be. And even though links sound a little complicated, they are extremely easy to create. The hardest part is deciding where you want a link to lead.

Tasks

Task #		Page #
1	Exploring How Links Work	52
2	Choosing Where the Links in Your Personal Page Point	54
3	Creating New Links from Scratch	56
4	Linking Your Own Pages to Each Other to Make a Web Site	58
5	Linking to a Particular Spot on a Page	60
6	Linking to Files So Your Visitors Can Download Them	62
7	Linking to Your Email So Visitors Can Contact You	64
8	Checking That Links Go Where They're Supposed To	66

Task 1: Exploring How Links Work

Every link has two parts: the *link source*—the object in the page that a visitor clicks to activate the link—and the *URL*—the address of the page to which the link takes the visitor. Creating links is really just a matter of creating the link source in your page, then adding the URL behind it. You can learn a lot more about links by studying the link sources and URLs on the pages you visit online.

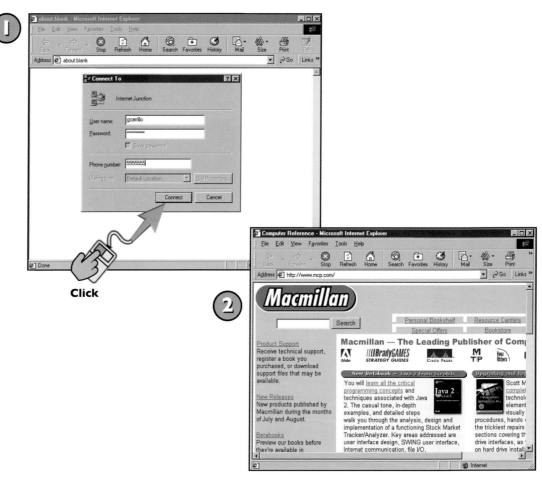

Click

✓ **Spotting Links**

When the link source is text, it usually appears underlined and in a unique color. When the link source is a picture, you can locate the link by pointing to the picture; if it's a link, the pointer becomes a pointing hand.

 Open your Web browser (Internet Explorer or Netscape Navigator) and connect to the Internet.

 Surf to a page you like that contains links.

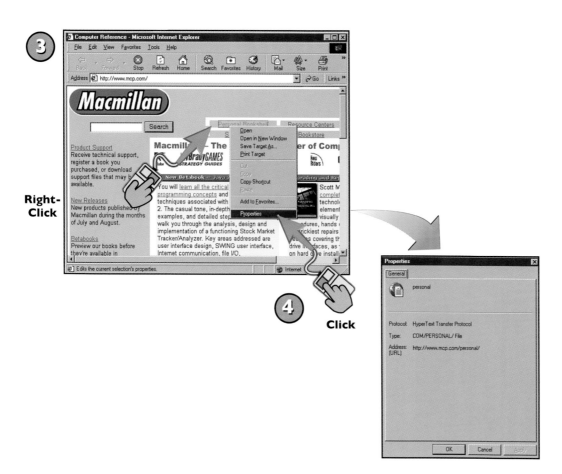

Right-Click

Click

3 Point to a link, in which the link source is text, and right-click it.

4 Choose **Properties**. The Properties dialog box shows the address (URL) to which the link points, along with other information.

✔ **Copying a Web Address**

You can copy a Web page address from the Properties dialog box by selecting the address, then right-clicking and choosing Copy. If you then go immediately to FrontPage Express to create a link in a page, you can paste the URL into the dialog box by clicking there and pressing Ctrl+V.

Task 2: Choosing Where the Links in Your Personal Page Point

If you used FrontPage Express's Personal Home Page Wizard to start a page (as described in Part 2), then your page already contains some links: the Hot List. But those links lead to phony addresses now. Here's how to make them point wherever you want.

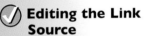 **Editing the Link Source**

You can, of course, edit the link source to change it from Sample Site to anything you like. But sometimes when you edit link source text, you inadvertently remove the link formatting—you change it from a link source to ordinary text. If that happens, just re-create the link, as described in the first few steps of Task 3. It only takes a couple of clicks.

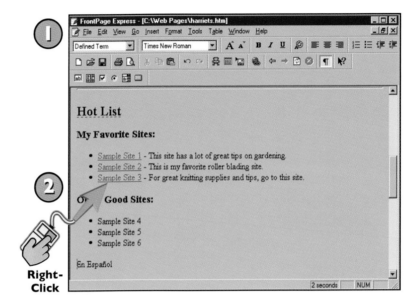

Right-Click

Decide on a Web site address you like. (If you need a suggestion, try **http://www.mcp.com**.)

Point to one of the Sample Site links listed in your Hot List. Right-click the **Sample Site** link.

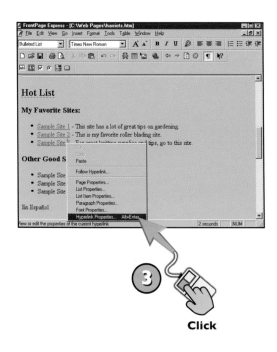

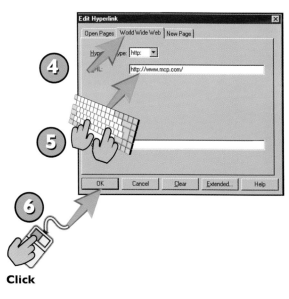

Click

Click

(3) Choose **Hyperlink Properties**.

(4) Be sure that the **World Wide Web** tab is selected.

(5) In the box labeled **URL**, type the complete URL. Be sure to include the **http://** part at the beginning.

(6) Click **OK**. The link source you pointed to in step 2 is now a link that points to the URL you chose.

✔ **Always Ask Permission to Link**
Before publishing a page that contains links to other Web sites, visit those Web sites and look for the email address of the person responsible for the site: the Webmaster. As a courtesy, email the Webmaster to ask if it's OK to publish a link to the site.

Task 3: Creating New Links from Scratch

In Task 2, you had a head start because the link source had already been created, so all you had to do was add the URL. Now it's time to create a link from scratch: source and URL together.

✓ **Formatting Links**
Although you can apply character formatting (such as fonts or italics) to the link source text you create, it's best not to. Browsers usually display link source text with standard formatting (usually blue and underlined) to help the visitor instantly identify links on a page. You don't want your character formatting to make finding links tricky for your visitors by changing the link source formatting they're accustomed to seeing.

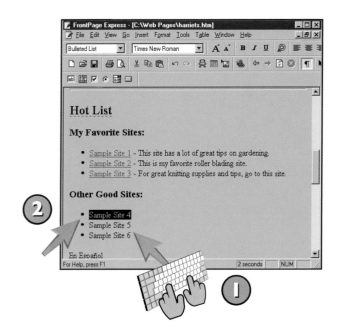

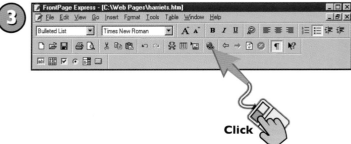

Click

① Type and format the text that will serve as the link source.

② Select the text.

③ Click the **Create or Edit Hyperlink** button on the Standard toolbar.

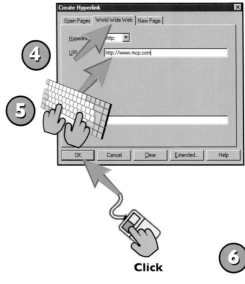

Click

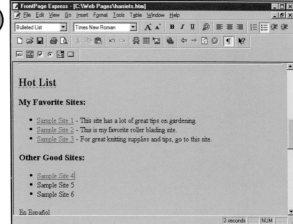

④ Be sure that the **World Wide Web** tab is selected.

⑤ In the box labeled **URL**, type the complete URL. Be sure to include the **http://** part at the beginning. Click **OK**.

⑥ The selected text becomes a hyperlink.

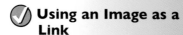

Using an Image as a Link

You can use a picture as a link source, so that clicking the picture activates the link. Doing so adds a lot of pizzazz to your pages. For example, you could use buttons or icons rather than text links (see **Part 5**).

Task 4: Linking Your Own Pages to Each Other to Make a Web Site

Ultimately, you might have more to say than can fit conveniently on a single page. So, you'll need to create a *Web site* made up of several pages that link together. Linking one of your own pages to other pages is a little different from linking elsewhere—but still easy.

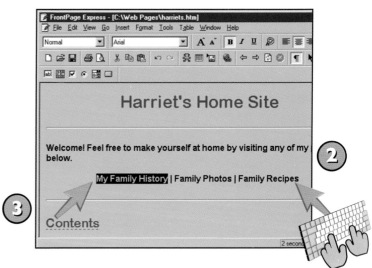

✓ Creating a Navigation Menu

One good way to link pages together is to create a string of links, containing a separate link for each page, and placing them at the bottom of every page. That way, your visitors can jump from any page in your Web site to any other, with just one click.

① Create the Web pages that will make up your Web site and save them all in the same folder.

② Type and format the text that will serve as the link sources.

③ Select the text of one link source.

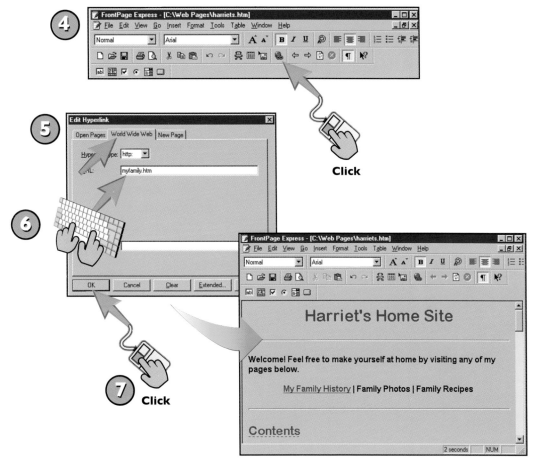

Click

End Task

④ Click the **Create or Edit Hyperlink** button on the Standard toolbar.

⑤ Be sure that the **World Wide Web** tab is selected.

⑥ In the box labeled **URL**, type the complete filename of the Web page you are linking to (including the **.htm** part). Do not put http:// or anything else at the beginning.

⑦ Click **OK**.

✓ **Don't Believe the Type**
When typing your page filename in the **URL** box, ignore the entry in the **Hyperlink Type** box. That entry automatically becomes **Other** when you click **OK**, which is what you want.

✓ **Store All the Files Together!**
When you publish this Web site, it will be important that you store all your Web page files in the same directory on the Web server.

Task 5: Linking to a Particular Spot on a Page

Links don't always lead to other pages or files. In a long or complex page, a link might lead to another part of the same page. If you created the **Personal Home Page** in Part 2, you might have noticed that the top of the page contains a **Contents** list of links, each of which jumps to a particular section of the page. That **Contents** list works because of *bookmarks*, such as the following ones that you are about to create.

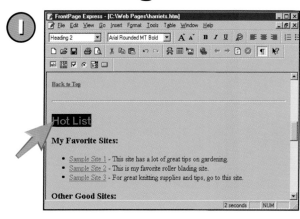

Click

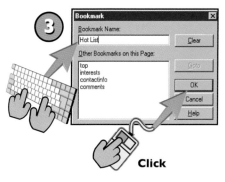

Click

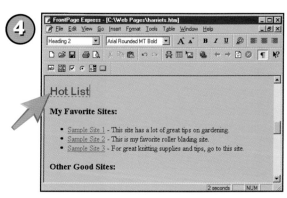

Using the Default Bookmark Name

In step 3, the text you selected in step 1 appears automatically as the bookmark name. You can leave that text alone and let it serve as the name, or change it to another name. Changing the bookmark name has no effect on the text in the page.

1. Select text at the spot where you want a bookmark.

2. Click **Edit**, then choose **Bookmark**.

3. Type a name for the bookmark and click **OK**.

4. Create the link source for a link to that bookmark.

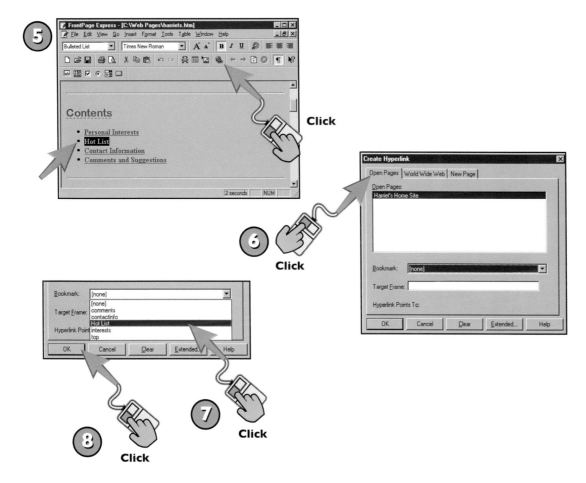

Click

Click

Click

Click

Click

Spotting Bookmarked Text
In FrontPage Express, a dashed line appears underneath text that has a bookmark attached. This is so that you can tell at a glance where your bookmarks are located. The underlining does not show up when the page is viewed through a browser.

⑤ Select the link source, then click the **Create or Edit Hyperlink** button on the Standard toolbar.

⑥ Click the **Open Pages** tab.

Playing the Name Game
FrontPage Express calls the spots you can link to within a page bookmarks. But different terms for the same thing are used outside of FrontPage. In some other Web authoring programs, bookmarks are called targets, and in HTML authoring (see Part 9) they're called anchors.

⑦ Click the **Bookmark** drop-down list and choose the bookmark name.

⑧ Click **OK**.

End Task

Task 6: Linking to Files So Your Visitors Can Download Them

You might have content that you want to offer your visitors, but don't want to turn into a Web page—for example, if you have a lengthy document, report, or other file. In that case, it might be better to provide that file for downloading instead of turning it into a Web page (or series of Web pages). You can provide any kind of computer file for downloading—documents, sound clips, pictures, and so on.

 Using Helper Programs

To use a file you provide, the visitor must have the same program. For example, if you publish a Word file, the visitor must have a program that can display (or convert) Word files to view it. You cannot do much about this, except to try to offer only popular, widely used file types, such as Word for documents, .avi for video clips (see Part 5), or .wav for sound clips.

 Locate the file you want to link to and move or copy it to the folder where your Web page files are stored.

 In the Web page, type and format the text that you want to use as the link source.

 Select the text of the link source.

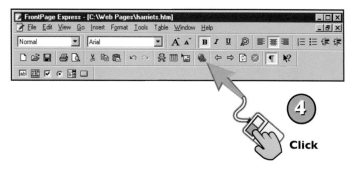

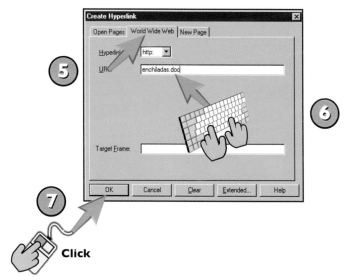

Click

Click

(4) Click the **Create or Edit Hyperlink** button on the Standard toolbar.

(5) Be sure that the **World Wide Web** tab is selected.

(6) In the box labeled **URL**, type the complete filename of the file. Do not put "http://" at the beginning.

(7) Click **OK**.

✓ **Always Provide the File Type and Size**
In the link source text (or right next to it), it's courteous to tell your visitors the file type so they can tell whether it's a file they are equipped to view. Providing the size of the file is also a good idea. That way, your viewers can guesstimate how long it will take to download at the speed of their Internet connection.

✓ **Did We Mention Storing the Files Together?**
When you publish this Web site, it is important that you store all your Web page files in the same directory on the Web server.

Task 7: Linking to Your Email So Visitors Can Contact You

Near the bottom of the Personal Home Page example, and in many pages you see online, a *signature* appears. A signature is text telling visitors who created (or manages) the page. Usually, a signature includes a *mailto* link, a link that points to the email address of the Web page author. If you add a signature and mailto link to your page, when a visitor clicks that link, his email program opens a new message, automatically preaddressed to you.

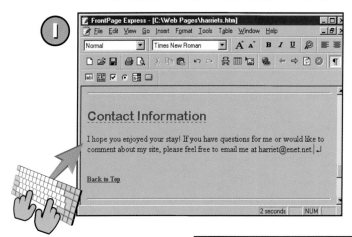

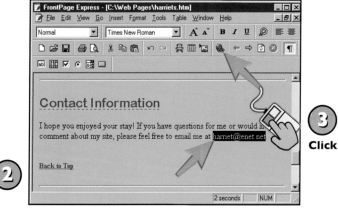

Click

① Near the bottom of your page (or in another easy-to-find spot), type a signature message such as the one shown.

② Select some text in the message—your name or email address—to serve as a link source for the mailto link.

③ Click the **Create or Edit Hyperlink** button on the Standard toolbar and be sure that the **World Wide Web** tab is selected.

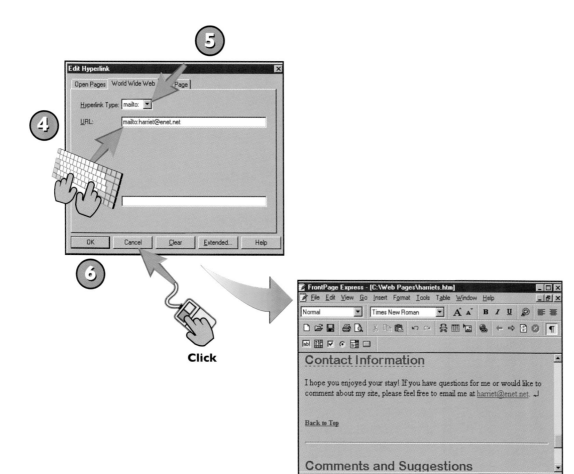

Click

Naming Your Mailto Link

The link source of a mailto link need not show your exact email address, because most visitor email programs will use the correct address automatically when they click the link. However, some visitors use Internet software that doesn't support mailto links; they see the link source, but nothing happens when they click it. So always include your exact email address somewhere in the signature.

4 In the box labeled **URL**, type your complete email address. Do not put http:// or anything else at the beginning.

5 In the Hyperlink Type box, choose **mailto:**. The word mailto appears right before your email address.

6 Click **OK**. The text becomes a mailto: link.

Task 8: Checking That Links Go Where They're Supposed To

When you create links that lead from your page to other pages online, the only way to be absolutely sure that links lead where they're supposed to is to test the links online—after you've published your page. However, you can do a pretty reliable prepublishing link check at any time, right from within FrontPage Express.

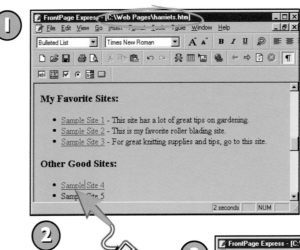

Start Here

Click

Click

✓ **You Can Test Your Links Offline...**

You don't need to connect to the Internet to test links to bookmarks or to files on your PC (such as other pages within a Web site you're creating but have not yet published). You can test those just by opening the page file in your browser and trying the links offline.

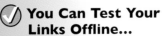

1 Connect to the Internet, open FrontPage Express, and open the page file in which you want to test the links.

2 Point to a link you want to test and click so that the edit cursor appears there.

3 Click **Tools**, then choose **Follow Hyperlink**.

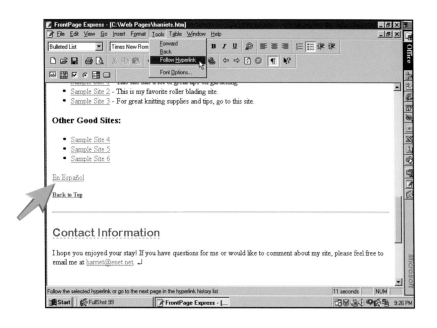

 (4) Be sure to test the other links on your page.

 ...But Test Them Again Online
Even if your links work, be certain to test them again, online, after you have published your page.

PART 5

Adding Style to Your Pages

Most of the hard stuff is over—filling your Web pages with text. Now comes the fun and creative part. In this part, you can explore unique ways to give your page style, including choosing colors, adding pictures, and even adding animation and sound.

One word of caution, though—a busy, over-styled Web page is an eyesore. Less is truly more in the case of Web design. Most visitors hit a page for its content, not its style. Although style is a nice addition, if it overwhelms the substance, you might lose more visitors than you gain. But that doesn't mean you can't be creative.

Colors, backgrounds, and horizontal lines help a page's appeal; there really is no impact on page's performance. However, every picture, sound, or animation you add to a page lengthens the time it takes the page to fully materialize on a visitor's screen. You know from your own surfing trips how frustrating a slow Web page is, especially when it's slow because it has too many pictures. So, my advice is to use style conservatively so as not to overdo it.

Tasks

Task #		Page #
1	Choosing Text Colors and Background Colors	70
2	Adding Lines to Divide Up a Page	72
3	Changing the Look of a Line	73
4	Finding Pictures	74
5	Copying a Picture from the Web	75
6	Creating Pictures	76
7	Giving a Picture a Transparent Background	78
8	Putting a Picture in a Page	79
9	Changing the Size of a Picture	80
10	Changing the Shape of a Picture	81
11	Putting a Border Around a Picture	82
12	Choosing a Picture's Alignment	83
13	Controlling How Text Aligns to a Picture	84
14	Using a Picture as a Link	85
15	Creating a Times Square–Style Animated Marquee	86
16	Adding a Picture Background	88
17	Finding and Adding Animations	90
18	Finding Sound Clips	91
19	Playing a Background Sound	92

Task 1: Choosing Text Colors and Background Colors

To add appeal, you can choose a *color scheme*, a group of colors that both contrast and complement one another. In creating your scheme, you pick the color for the background, text, links, *visited links* (links the visitor has used already), and *active links* (links the visitor has just clicked, but which still appear onscreen briefly while the link is being activated).

✓ Jazzing Up Your Background
Instead of a solid color background, you can use an image as a background (see Task 16).

✓ Ensuring Good Contrast
Be careful that all your selected text and link colors stand out against the background. For example, if you select a dark background color, all the text colors must be light so that the text will be legible. You can adjust all these options from the Background tab.

Start Here

Click

Click

1. Open a Web page for which you want to choose colors.

2. Click **File**, and then choose **Page Properties**.

3. Click the **Background** tab.

Next Step

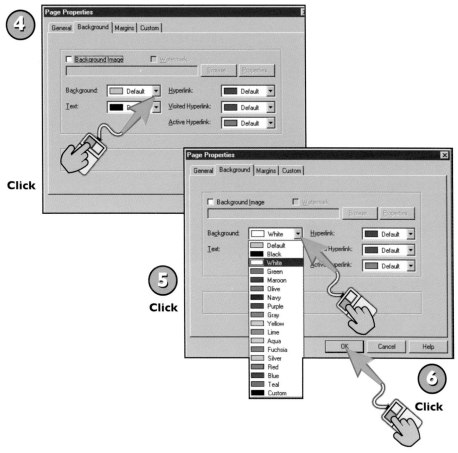

Click

Click

Click

④ Click the arrow on the **Background** drop-down list to display your color options.

⑤ Click the color you want to use for the background.

⑥ Repeat steps 4 and 5 for the other color lists. Click **OK**.

✓ **Allowing Default Colors**
Choosing **Default** from a color list assigns no color. It allows the color for that object to be determined by the color settings in the visitor's browser. Because the color the browser chooses might not show up properly with other colors you've selected, never pick Default unless you pick Default for all colors in the page.

✓ **Creating Custom Colors**
In the color lists, the Custom choice opens a dialog box from which you can create and select a different color from those already shown in the list.

Task 2: Adding Lines to Divide Up a Page

Horizontal lines help to visually divide up a page. Used between a heading and the paragraph that follows it, a line can add a little extra style to page. Lines also help divide sections of a longer page.

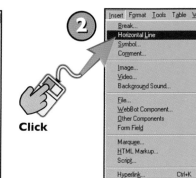

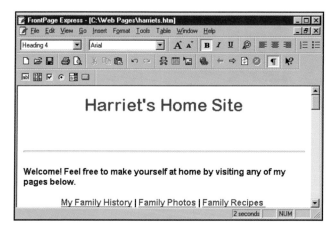

Using Fancier Lines
You might see fancy, multicolor lines dividing some pages. These aren't real lines; they're pictures, used like lines. You can find these pictures in clip art libraries (see Task 4) in categories with names like Bars or Rules, and you insert them like any other picture (see Task 8).

1 Click on the page where you want to insert the line.

2 Click **Insert**, then choose **Horizontal Line**. The line appears on your page.

Task 3: Changing the Look of a Line

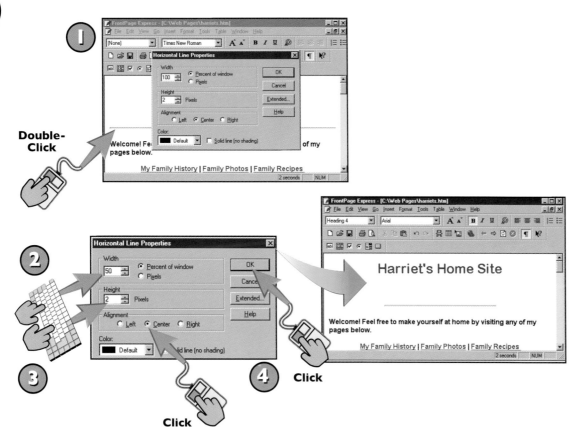

Double-Click

Click

Click

Click

Now that you have a horizontal line in place, you can change its appearance by making it thicker, thinner, shorter, or changing its alignment on the page.

① Double-click a line.

② To make the line shorter than the full width of the page, in **Width** type a percentage figure less than 100.

③ In **Height**, type a number to change the thickness of the line; a higher number makes a thicker line.

④ Select the Alignment (**Left**, **Right**, or **Center**) you want, the line **Color**, and click **OK**.

✓ **Determining Line Width**
In the Horizontal Line Properties dialog box, always leave the **Percent of Window** option selected, so that the number you type in **Width** expresses the width as a percentage of the page's width. Choosing the other option might produce unpredictable results on visitor screens.

End Task

Task 4: Finding Pictures

Nearly all the images you see on Web pages are in the **GIF** file type. Some images are in **JPEG** format, mostly photographs. But any pictures used in your Web pages must be in one of these two formats. You can create your own pictures (see Task 6), but you can also pick up great pictures from clip art libraries on **CD** or online.

✓ **Paying the Clip Art Piper**
Some clip art you must pay for, some is free, and some is free with strings attached. Always read and follow all copyright notices and other usage instructions on any page from which you download clip art or other files you plan to use.

✓ **Locating Clip Art Treasures**
A good way to find tons of clip art sites is to do a search with Yahoo! (**www.yahoo.com**), Excite (**www.excite.com**) or another search page, using **Web Clip Art** as a search term.

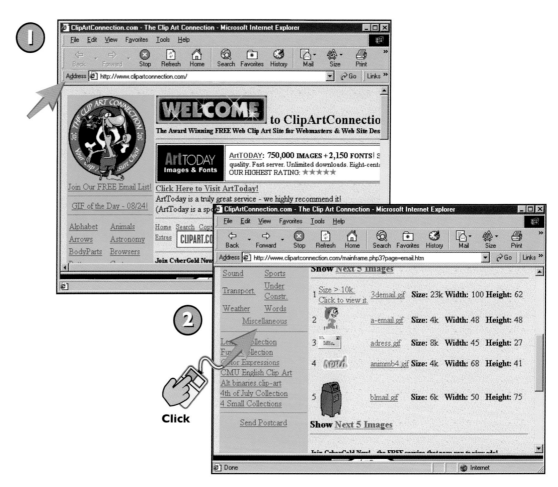

Click

In your Web browser, go to a good online clip art library or site. If you don't know which one to choose, use **www.clipartconnection.com** for starters.

Click through the categories to locate an image you want to use.

Task 5: Copying a Picture from the Web

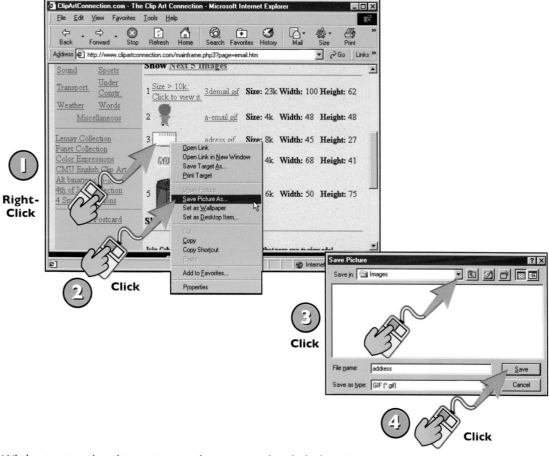

Right-Click ①

Click ②

Click ③

Click ④

When you locate a clip art picture online that you want to use, you can copy it to a folder on your PC (shown in the following steps), and use it later to insert on your Web pages (as shown in Task 8).

① While viewing the clip art in your browser, right-click the picture.

② Choose **Save Picture As** (if you browse in Internet Explorer) or **Save Image As** (if you browse in Netscape Navigator).

③ Open the **Save In** list and choose the folder that contains your Web page files.

④ Click **Save**.

✓ Using CD-ROM Clip Art
If the picture you want to use is in a clip art library you obtained on a floppy disk or **CD-ROM**, always copy the picture file from there to the folder where your Web page files are stored, and then insert the picture as shown in Task 8.

Task 6: Creating Pictures

You can create your own Web page pictures with almost any draw or paint program you might have. In fact, Paint—the program built into Windows—works perfectly for beginners.

✓ **Learning More About Paint**
To learn how to paint a picture in Windows Paint, open Paint, click **Help**, and click **Help Topics**.

✓ **Using Your Own Pictures**
To get your own photographs into your Web pages, scan them with a scanner, take them to a computer graphics shop to be scanned, or take them with a digital camera. Use the scanner or camera software to save the image as a GIF or JPEG file and store it in the same folder as your other Web page files. You can even have picture disks created when you get your film developed.

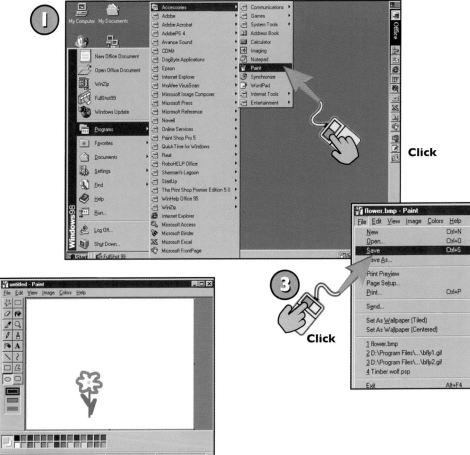

① Click **Start**, then choose **Programs**, **Accessories**, and **Paint**.

② Use Paint's tools to create your masterpiece.

③ When you are finished creating your masterpiece, be sure to save it. Click **File**, then choose **Save**.

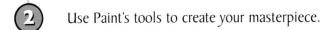

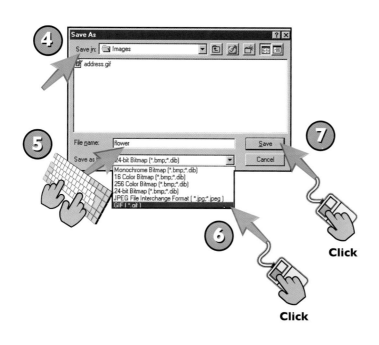

Click

Click

✓ **Converting Other Graphics Formats**

If you use a draw, paint, or scan program that can't optionally save files in GIF or JPEG format, you can still use the picture. FrontPage Express can automatically convert most other common picture file formats—including .BMP, .PCX, and .TIFF—to GIF. Just save in one of those formats and let FrontPage Express handle the conversion.

(4) Use the **Save In** list to select the folder where you store the Web page in which you will use this picture.

(5) Type a short **File Name** for your creation. Don't type a *filename extension* (a period and three letters at the end).

(6) Click the **Save as Type** drop-down list and choose **GIF (*.gif)**.

(7) Click **Save**.

End Task

Task 7: Giving a Picture a Transparent Background

Using your draw, paint, or image-editing software, you can give your GIF pictures a "transparent" background; without a transparent background, the picture appears to have a rectangular, colored background. A transparent background removes the colored rectangle, allowing the page's background to show through. Here's how to choose transparency in Paint.

✓ Choosing a Transparent Color
If parts of the picture are the same as the background color, they too become transparent when you perform step 3. To prevent this, between steps 2 and 3, click the **Select Color** button and choose a color not used elsewhere in your picture.

✓ Viewing the Transparent Color
After you insert the picture (see Task 8), the background will not look transparent in FrontPage Express. To see your GIF as visitors will see it, view the page through your browser.

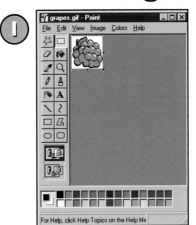

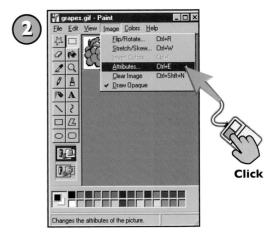

Click

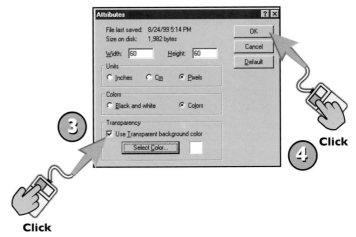

Click

Click

① In Paint, open a picture you've saved in GIF format.

② Click **Image**, then choose **Attributes**.

③ In the Transparency section, select the check box next to **Use Transparent Background Color**.

④ Click **OK**.

Task 8: Putting a Picture in a Page

Start
Here

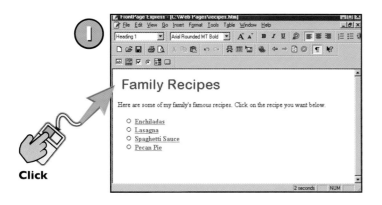

Click

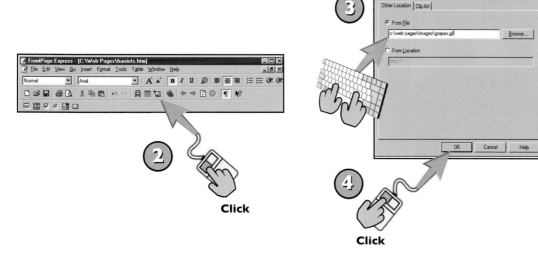

Click

Click

Click

When you have your **GIF** or **JPEG** image ready to go, just drop it in your page, right where you want it. It's important to start with the picture file stored in the same folder as your Web page file. This not only makes inserting the picture easier, but also makes publishing easier when it comes time to publish your Web pages, as you learn in Part 7.

✅ **Moving Images**
To move a picture after inserting it, just point to it, click and hold, drag to the new spot, and then release. Or, select the picture, click the **Cut** button, click in the new spot, and click the **Paste** button.

✅ **Inserting Other Image Formats**
If the picture you want to insert is not in GIF or JPEG format, you can still insert it by typing its filename in step 3. When you save the Web page, FrontPage Express automatically converts the file to GIF format.

① Click in your page at the spot where you want to insert the picture.

② Click the **Insert Image** button on the Standard toolbar.

③ Type the filename of the picture or click **Browse** to locate it.

④ Click **OK**.

End
Task

Task 9: Changing the Size of a Picture

After inserting a picture, you can change its size within FrontPage Express.

Start Here

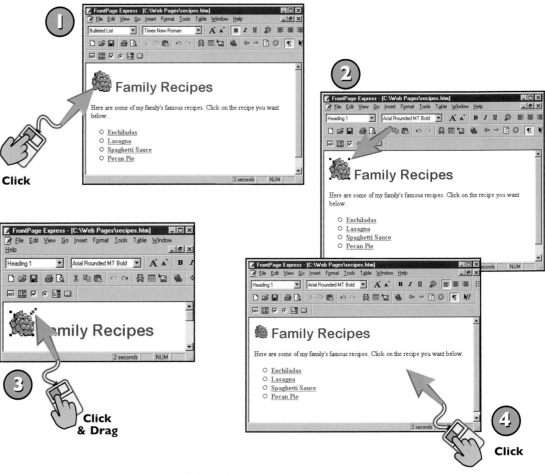

Click

Click & Drag

Click

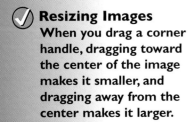

✓ Resizing Images
When you drag a corner handle, dragging toward the center of the image makes it smaller, and dragging away from the center makes it larger.

1. Click on the picture to select it. **Handles**—little squares—appear around the picture to show that it is selected.

2. Point to a handle on a corner—**not** a side or the top or bottom—of the picture.

3. Click and hold on the corner handle, and drag to resize the image.

4. Click anywhere else in the page to deselect the picture.

End Task

Task 10: Changing the Shape of a Picture

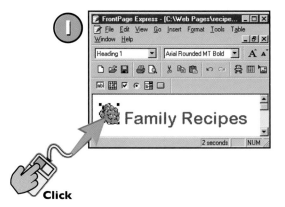

Click

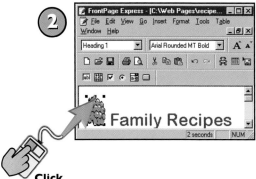

Click

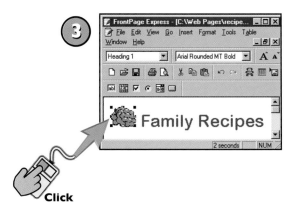

Click

Click

In Task 9, you were told to only drag the corner handles of an image to resize it. That is because the corner handles automatically resize the height and width proportionately, so that the image retains its basic shape and appearance. However, when working with abstract shapes or going for a special effect, you can drag the handles on the top, bottom, or sides to change the shape of the image, stretching or squeezing (and distorting) it.

1. Click on the picture to select it.

2. To stretch or squash the picture vertically, drag a top or bottom handle.

3. To widen or narrow the picture horizontally, drag a side handle.

4. Click anywhere else in the page to deselect the picture.

✓ Undoing Mistakes
If you decide you don't like the way you changed the shape of the image, use the **Undo Clear** button to restore the image to its original size and shape.

End
Task

Task 11: Putting a Border Around a Picture

To give an image a more polished look, you can put a border around it.

✓ **Selecting Border Size**
Typing "2" in **Border Thickness** makes a simple, bold border. A lower number makes a finer border; a higher number, a thicker one. A border thicker than 10 is probably overkill. A border of 0 is no border at all—some Web sites eliminate the border from images that are used for links.

✓ **Spacing Your Images**
On the **Appearance** tab, you have boxes for choosing Horizontal Spacing and Vertical Spacing. Raising the numbers in these boxes adds extra space between the image (or the image border, if you've added one) and whatever is next to it. Increasing vertical spacing adds space above and below the image; increasing horizontal spacing adds space to the left and right of the image.

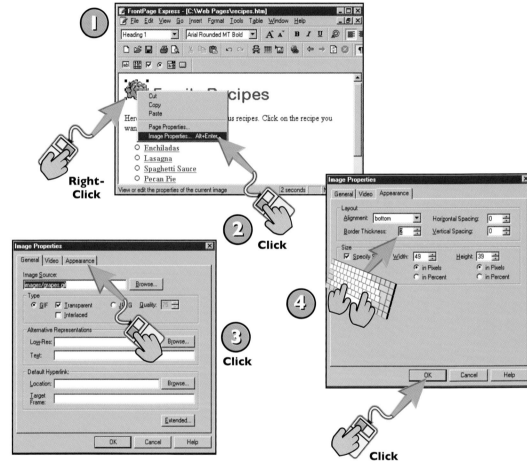

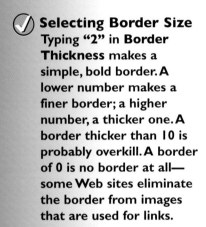

1. Right-click on the picture.

2. Choose **Image Properties**.

3. Click the **Appearance** tab.

4. In **Border Thickness**, type a number to add the border, then click **OK**.

Task 12: Choosing a Picture's Alignment

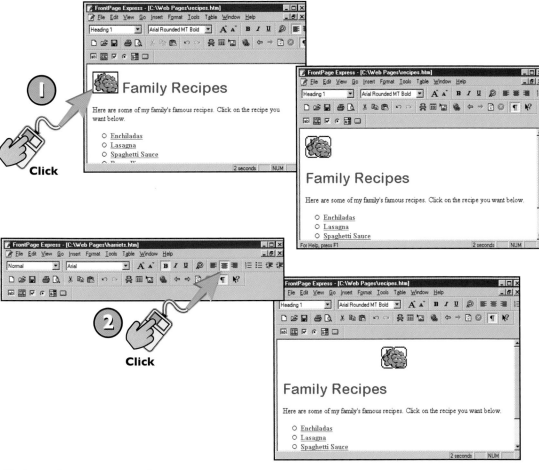

By default, any picture you insert goes on the left side of the page. But you can center it or align it to the right side of the page, exactly as you do text.

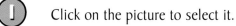

Click on the picture to select it.

From the Formatting toolbar, click the **Align Left**, **Center**, or **Align Right** button.

When you use images around text, you have control of the relationship between the text and picture. You can choose to start text below the image, to the right of it, or to the left of it.

Task 13: Controlling How Text Aligns to a Picture

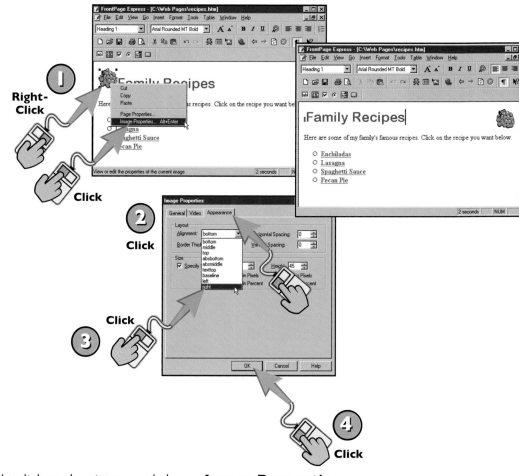

Right-Click

Click

Click

Click

Click

Aligning Your Images with Text

There are too many text alignment options to show each one here, but the most important choices are: top (text aligns to the upper-right corner of the image), bottom (text at lower-right corner of the image), middle (text at the middle of the right side of the image), and right (the image goes to the right of the text).

① Right-click on the picture, and choose **Image Properties**.

② Click the **Appearance** tab.

③ Click the **Alignment** drop-down list and choose the alignment you want to apply.

④ Click **OK**.

Task 14: Using a Picture as a Link

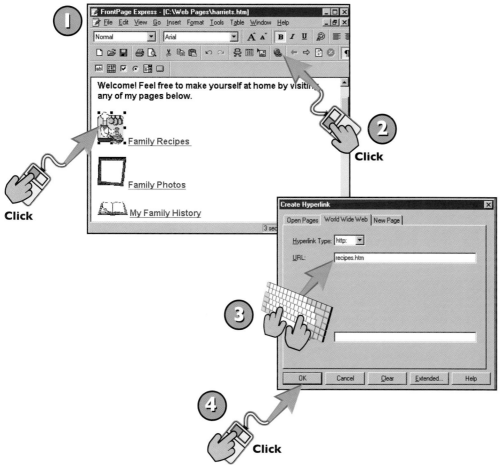

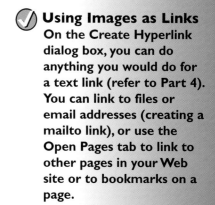

Using a picture as a *link source*—the thing a visitor clicks to activate a link (refer to **Part 4**)—is just like using text as a link source. The only difference is that you start out by selecting a picture, not text.

Click

Click

Click

Click

1   Click on the picture you want to make into a link to select it.

2   Click the **Create Hyperlink** button on the Standard toolbar.

3   From the World Wide Web tab, type the URL of the page or file to which this link leads.

4   Click **OK**.

✓ **Using Images as Links**
On the **Create Hyperlink** dialog box, you can do anything you would do for a text link (refer to **Part 4**). You can link to files or email addresses (creating a mailto link), or use the **Open Pages** tab to link to other pages in your Web site or to bookmarks on a page.

Task 15: Creating a Times Square–Style Animated Marquee

A *marquee* is a short slice of animated text that scrolls through a Web page. The effect is like the scrolling marquee on the *New York Times* building in Manhattan, the one people in movies are always watching for bulletins during a crisis. Marquees are a fast way to add a little action to a page and are usually used for text you really want the visitor to notice.

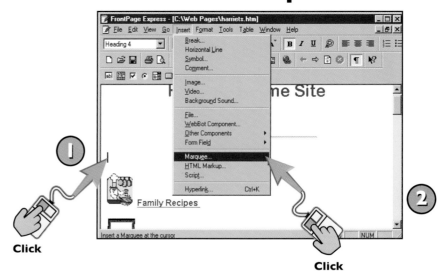

Click

Click

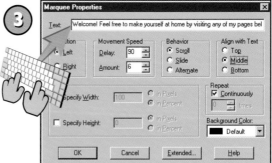

✓ Marquees Are Not Universal

At this writing, scrolling marquees are supported in Internet Explorer, but not in Netscape Navigator. Navigator users will see your marquee text as regular, static text on the page.

(1) Click the page at the spot where you want to insert your scrolling marquee.

(2) Click **Insert**, and then choose **Marquee**.

(3) Type the text you want to see scrolling along.

Next Step

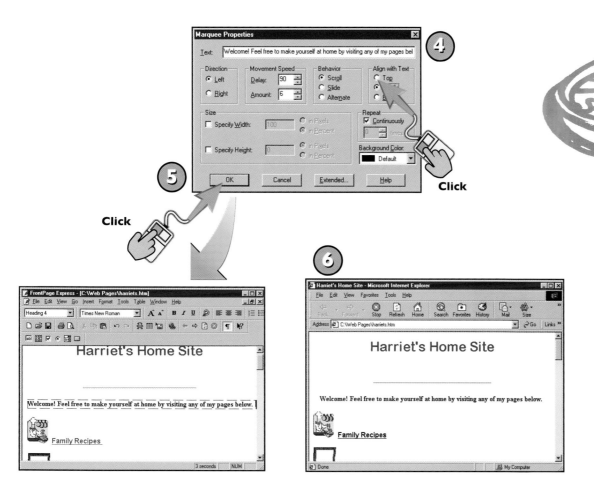

Click

Click

④ You can use the default options for **Direction**, **Speed**, and so on, or make any changes to these settings you desire.

⑤ Click **OK**. The marquee text appears in FrontPage Express as a fixed, ordinary heading.

⑥ View the page in Internet Explorer to see the marquee scroll as it will to visitors who use Internet Explorer.

✓ **Changing Text Options**
To change the options or text for a scrolling marquee, just double-click on the marquee to open the **Marquee Properties** dialog box, change whatever you like, and then click **OK**.

Task 16: Adding a Picture Background

Instead of using a solid color background, as you learned to do in Task 1, you can use a picture as a background. If the picture is too small to fill the whole window in which the page appears, it is automatically *tiled*—repeated—to fill the window.

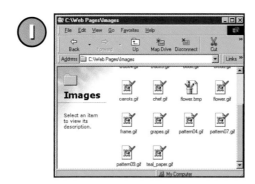

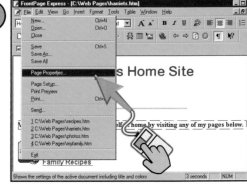

Click

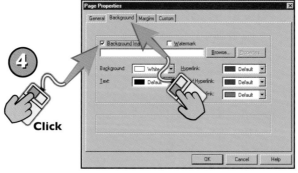

Click

Click

✓ Finding Background Images

You can get background image files that are specially designed so that, when tiled, they form a seamless texture, such as marble or wood. In clip art libraries, look for such images under categories labeled **Backgrounds** or **Textures**. You can also save the background of any Web page you visit by pointing to the background, right-clicking, and choosing the **Save** command from the resulting pop-up menu.

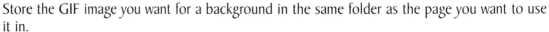

Store the GIF image you want for a background in the same folder as the page you want to use it in.

In FrontPage Express, open the page you want to add a background to, click **File**, and choose **Page Properties**.

Click the **Background** tab.

Click the check box next to **Background Image** to place a check mark there.

Next Step

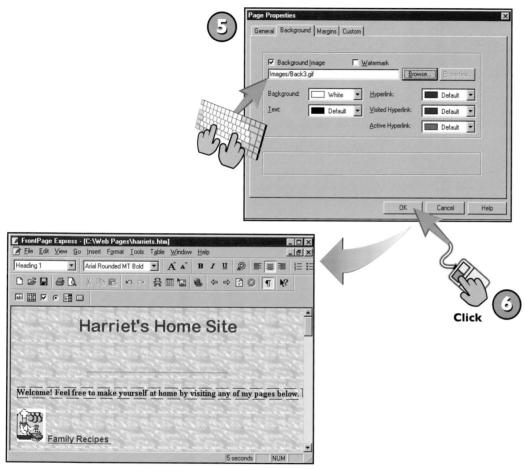

5 Click in the box beneath Background Image and type the filename of the GIF image you want to use.

6 Click **OK**.

✅ **Images Override Background Colors**
An image background automatically supercedes a background color. If you create an image background, any selection you might have made for background color is irrelevant.

✅ **Keeping Pages Up to Speed**
An image background, like any picture file, slows down the download of your page to the visitor, so watch out for using very large background files. A large background image can slow the page down more than a small, tiled picture.

Task 17: Finding and Adding Animations

A special kind of GIF image file, called an *animated GIF*, plays a brief, simple animation when you view it in a Web page. A good way to find Web sites offering animated GIFs is to do a search with Yahoo (www.yahoo.com), Excite (www.excite.com), or another search page, using `animated gif` as a search term.

✓ Viewing the Animation

Because FrontPage Express cannot play animated GIFs, you'll have to view it in Internet Explorer to see the animation in action.

✓ Creating Animated GIFs

You can create your own animated GIFs by creating a small series (6–12) of separate GIF images, each of which is a frame of the animation. Then you use a program, such as **GIF Construction Set**, to combine the frames into one animated GIF.

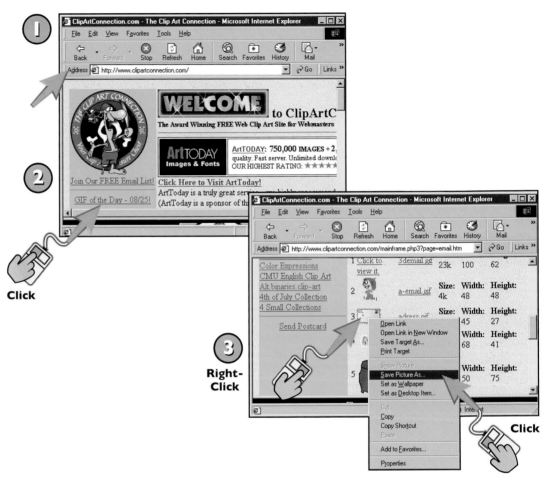

Start Here

Click

Right-Click

Click

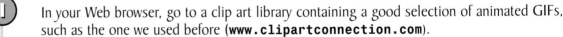

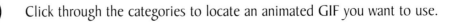

(1) In your Web browser, go to a clip art library containing a good selection of animated GIFs, such as the one we used before (www.clipartconnection.com).

(2) Click through the categories to locate an animated GIF you want to use.

(3) Copy the GIF to your PC and insert it in a Web page exactly as you would any GIF image (refer to Tasks 5 and 8).

End Task

Task 18: Finding Sound Clips

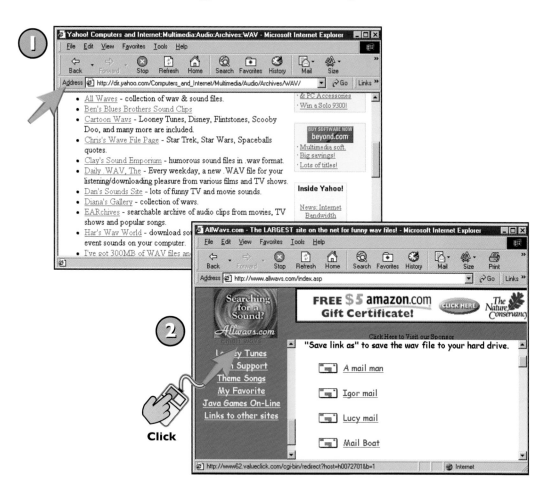

Click

A variety of different sound file formats are used on the Web. But for Windows users, the easiest type to deal with is .wav, known as *Wave*. Wave files (and other popular sound-file formats, such as .AU and .MID), are available in sound-clip libraries online or on CD-ROM. You can download sounds to your PC, then use them in your Web pages two ways: as background sounds or as a file to which a link leads, so that a visitor can choose to play the sound by clicking the link.

✓ **Record Your Own Voice Greeting**
Using your PC's sound card and a microphone, you can record your own Wave files. Most sound cards include their own audio recording program.

✓ **Finding Sound Clips**
You can search for sound clips in the same way you search for clip art. Also, sound clips are found on related sites.

1 In your Web browser, go to a sound-clip archive, like those listed here in the Yahoo! directory (**www.yahoo.com**).

2 Click through the categories to locate an image you want to use.

Task 19: Playing a Background Sound

A background sound is a sound clip that plays automatically when the visitor arrives at the page. You can add a background sound to a page in FrontPage Express, and choose whether that sound should play once, several times, or repeatedly.

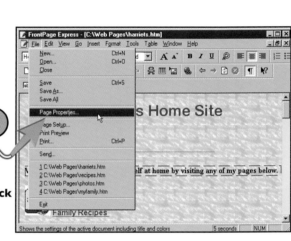

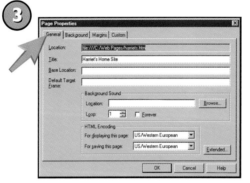

 Get (or create) a short Wave or MIDI file you want to use as a background sound and store it in the same folder in which your Web page files are stored.

 In FrontPage Express, open the page you want to add the sound to, click **File**, and choose **Page Properties**.

 Be sure the **General** tab is selected.

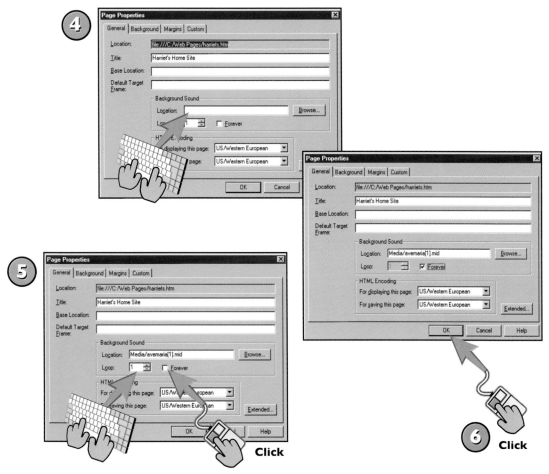

In the Background Sound section of the dialog box, click in the box labeled **Location** and type the filename of the Wave or MIDI file.

In **Loop**, type the number of times you want the sound to repeat, or check the check box next to **Forever** to make the sound play for as long as the visitor views the page.

Click **OK**.

Click

Click

✓ **Speak Up!**
Be sure your speakers are on to hear the background sound using Internet Explorer.

✓ **Don't Repeat Yourself**
As a rule, most sound effects or snips of speech are annoying if played more than once, so for these, type 1 in the **Loop** box. Some music clips or other sounds might be nice if kept playing; for them, you can click the **Forever** check box to play the sound continuously.

PART 6

Creating Tables and Forms

Like word-processing programs, creating Web pages with FrontPage Express offers tools for organizing content in attractive ways: headings, lists, indentation, alignment, horizontal lines, and wrapping around pictures. However, if you need to organize a lot of content (eight or more items) that fall logically into groups, using a table to display the content is the way to go. In this part, you discover not only how to make tables but some nice techniques on how to make them look good, too.

Before you leave this part, you also get an introduction to a technique that doesn't simply organize information, but actually collects it from your visitors: a *form*.

Tasks

Task #		Page #
1	Inserting a New Table	96
2	Putting Text in Table Cells	97
3	Putting Pictures in a Table	98
4	Adding a Caption to a Table	100
5	Dressing Up Tables with Borders	101
6	Choosing Custom Border Colors	102
7	Choosing a Background for a Table	103
8	Creating an Interactive Form	104

Task 1: Inserting a New Table

All you need to get started using tables is a page in progress, a rough idea of what you want to put in the table, and a rough idea of where you want to put it.

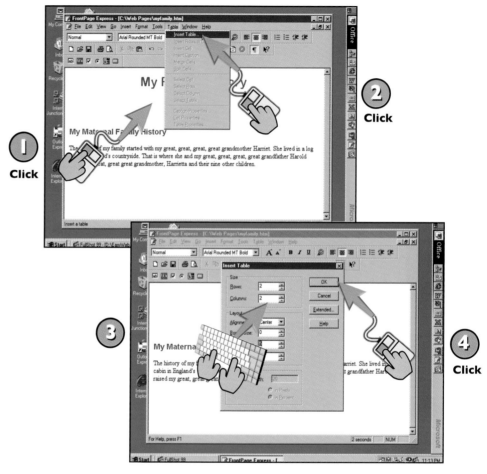

✓ Determining Rows and Columns

If you are not sure of how many rows and columns you will need, simply guess. You can always add more or remove some later.

✓ Don't Worry About the Table Borders

The dashed lines that show the table borders and gridlines appear just to show you where your table is—they don't show up when the page is viewed through a browser. A table without borders still organizes its contents into rows and columns. If you really want visible borders, see Task 5.

✓ Sizing Rows and Columns

Don't worry about the size of the rows and columns. As you put text into the cells, the rows and columns will expand to fit whatever you put in them.

Click

Click

2 **Click**

3

4 **Click**

1 Click the spot in your page where you want to insert the table.

2 Click **Table**, then choose **Insert Table**.

3 In **Rows** and **Columns**, choose the number of rows and columns you want for the table.

4 Click **OK**.

End
Task

Task 2: Putting Text in Table Cells

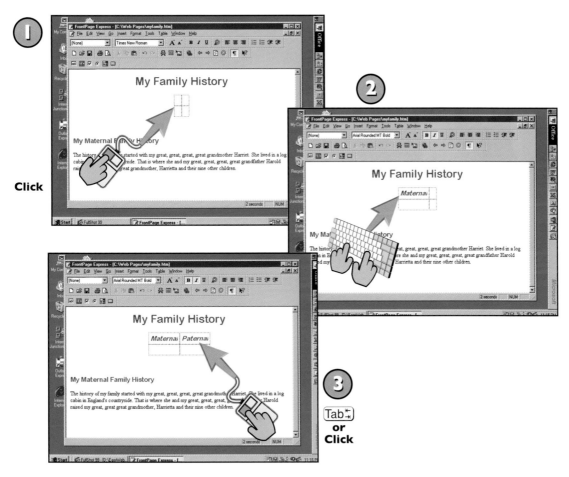

Click

Tab ⇄
or
Click

A table without content is like a house without furniture. Here's how to start filling in your new table by putting text in *cells*—the boxes formed by the walls of each row and column.

✅ **Formatting Table Text**
You can apply to text in a table any of the character formatting from Part 3, including fonts, sizes, bold, italic, underlining, or a special color. Making the text in all cells of the top row bold, italic, or a unique color is a nice way to create column headings that stand out.

✅ **Aligning Table Text**
If you apply alignment (refer to Part 3) to text in a cell, the text is aligned relative to the cell it's in, not the page. For example, if you apply center alignment to text in a cell, the text is centered within that cell only. Other cells are not affected.

① Click in the cell in which you want to type.

② Type whatever you want.

③ Press the **Tab** key to jump to the next cell (or click in the cell you want to fill next).

Task 3: Putting Pictures in a Table

Most tables are mostly text. But you are not limited to only using text in tables. You can give your table added panache by using pictures.

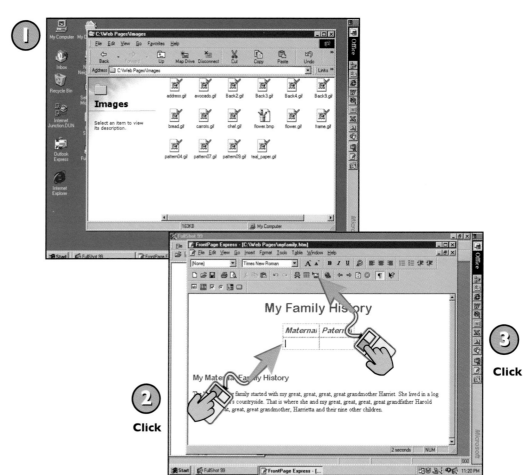

Adding Links to a Table

You can also put links in a table. Just add to the table the text or picture you want to use as the link source, highlight that text or picture in its table cell, and create the link as usual (refer to Part 4). Actually, a table makes a lot of sense for a list of links; it lets you organize them and even add comments or graphics, such as ratings or new site flags.

 Prepare the GIF or JPEG image you want to insert (refer to Part 5), and store it in the same folder as the Web page file that contains the table.

 Click in the cell in which you want to put a picture.

 Click the **Insert Image** button on the Standard toolbar.

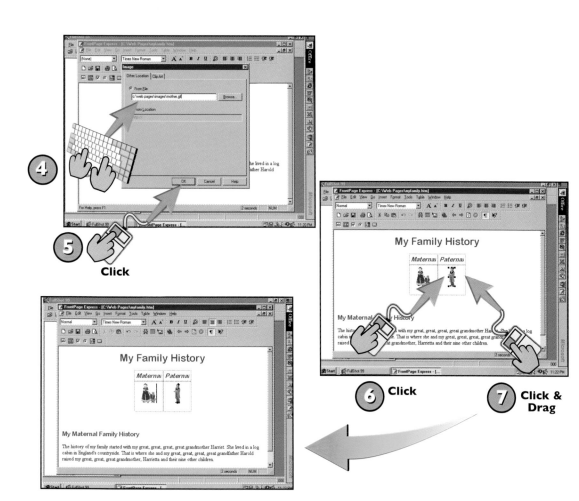

Click

Click

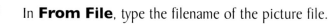

**Click &
Drag**

✓ **Formatting Pictures in
a Table**
You can use any of the
picture formatting
techniques from Part 5 on
a picture in a table cell. To
open the Image Properties
dialog box to format a
picture in a cell, point to
the picture, right-click, and
choose **Image Properties**
from the pop-up menu.

④ In **From File**, type the filename of the picture file.

⑤ Click **OK**.

⑥ Continue adding pictures to cells until you've added all the pictures for this table.

⑦ On each picture, drag a sizing handle (refer to Part 5) to scale the picture to the size you
desire. The row and column sizes automatically change to fit.

Task 4: Adding a Caption to a Table

If needed, you can add a **caption** (a descriptive title directly above or below the cells) to clarify or give instruction.

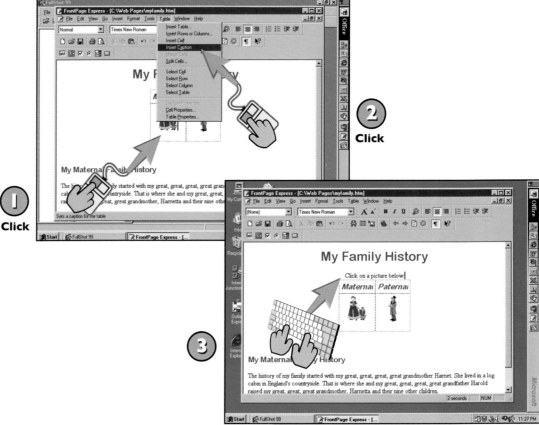

Click

Click

✓ **Adding Captions to a Table**

FrontPage Express automatically puts captions above the table, but you can move a caption below the table, too. Click anywhere on the caption, click **Table**, and then choose **Caption Properties**. A dialog box appears, giving you two choices for caption placement: **Top of Table** and **Bottom of Table**. Choose the one you want and click **OK**.

① Click anywhere in the table.

② Click **Table** and choose **Insert Caption**.

③ Type your caption. It appears above the table.

End
Task

Task 5: Dressing Up Tables with Borders

Start Here

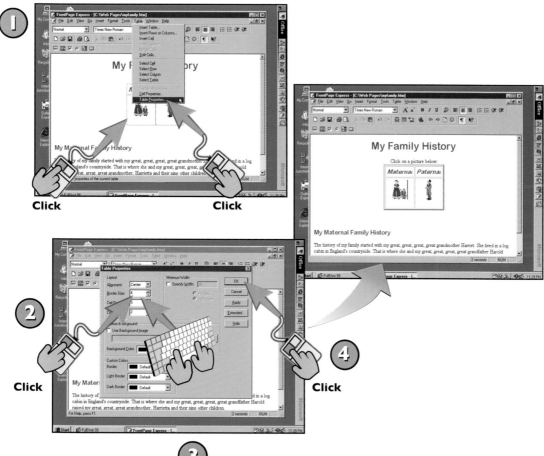

So far, you've learned how to use a table to line up content in rows and columns. But you might feel something is lacking— possibly lines to delineate the content and make the table look sharp.

① Click anywhere in the table, click **Table**, and then choose **Table Properties**.

② Click the box next to **Border Size**.

③ Type a number for the width of the borders. For example, type **4** to create a border 4 pixels wide. The higher the number, the thicker the border.

④ Click **OK**.

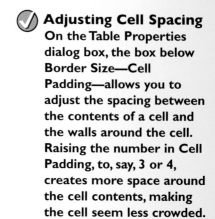 **Adjusting Cell Spacing**
On the Table Properties dialog box, the box below Border Size—Cell Padding—allows you to adjust the spacing between the contents of a cell and the walls around the cell. Raising the number in Cell Padding, to, say, 3 or 4, creates more space around the cell contents, making the cell seem less crowded.

End Task

Task 6: Choosing Custom Border Colors

Start Here

A table border is not one line, but three lines, used together to create a 3D effect. These lines are: a basic border line, a light border (a highlight on the top of horizontal lines and on the left side of vertical lines), and a dark border (a shadow on the bottom of horizontal lines and on the right side of vertical lines). You can choose the color for each part of the border.

✓ **Trying On Different Looks**

To experiment with borders, border colors, and anything else on the Table Properties dialog box, make any changes on the dialog box, then click the **Apply** button instead of **OK**. The changes are made in the table, but the Table Properties dialog box remains open, so you can try different settings without having to reopen it. Keep experimenting, clicking **Apply** each time, and then click **OK** when you see the combination you want to keep.

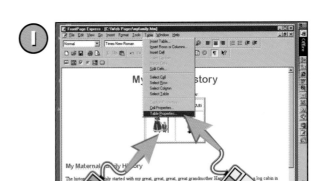

Click   Click

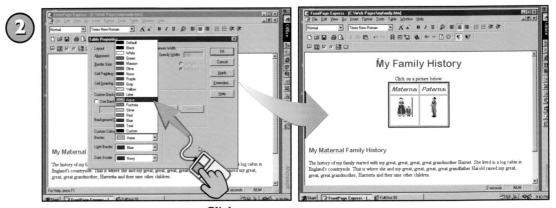

Click

1. Click anywhere in the table, click **Table**, and then choose **Table Properties**.

2. In the Custom Colors section, choose a color from each of the three lists: **Border**, **Light Border**, and **Dark Border**.

End Task

Task 7: Choosing a Background for a Table

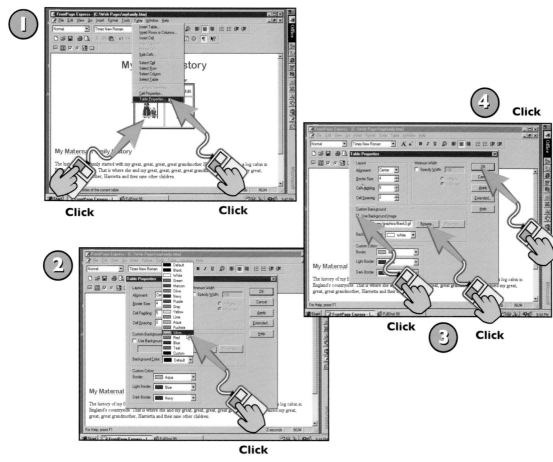

1

Click   Click

2

Click

4 Click

3 Click   Click

Unless you add a background to a table, the page's background color or image shows through the table (but does not obscure the table's content or borders). But a table can have its own background, different from that of the page, to make the table—and more importantly, its contents—really stand out.

✓ **Alternating Background Schemes in a Table**
You can use a different background for selected cells; for example, to make column headings stand out. In step 1, click in a cell, click **Table**, and then choose **Select Cell**, **Select Row**, or **Select Column**.

✓ **Background Images Override Color**
If you choose both a background image and a background color, the background image overrides the background color. However, you want to choose a background color that is close to the color of your background image, so your table text will show up even before the image loads.

1 Click anywhere in the table, click **Table**, and then choose **Table Properties**.

2 To add a solid color background, open the list next to **Background Color** and choose a color.

3 To add a picture background instead of a background color, click the check box next to **Use Background Image**. Then type the name of the GIF image, or **Browse** for it.

4 Click **OK**.

Task 8: Creating an Interactive Form

A *form* is a page that collects information from your visitors by prompting them to select options from lists, check check boxes, enter text, and more. While this *Easy* book can't effectively show you how to create forms from scratch, it can show you how to use the Form Page Wizard to create your own form.

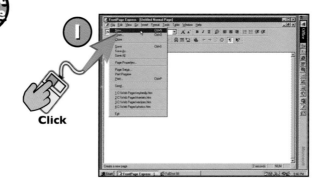

Click

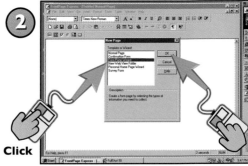

Click

Click

Click

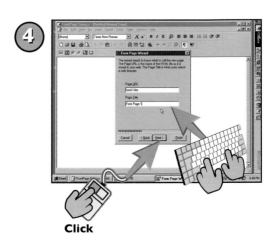

Click

✅ Inserting Fields on the Fly

You can use the buttons on the Forms toolbar to insert *form fields*—list boxes, check boxes, and so on—in any Web page. Just click in the page where you want the form field, click the button, and answer any questions FrontPage Express asks.

✅ Choosing the Right Form Tool

For a beginner, using the Form Page Wizard makes more sense than using the Forms toolbar. The wizard helps organize and encode your form correctly.

① From FrontPage Express, click **File** and choose **New**.

② Click **Form Page Wizard**, then click **OK**.

③ Click **Next**.

④ In the **Page URL** and **Page Title** boxes, type a filename and title, and click **Next**.

Next Step

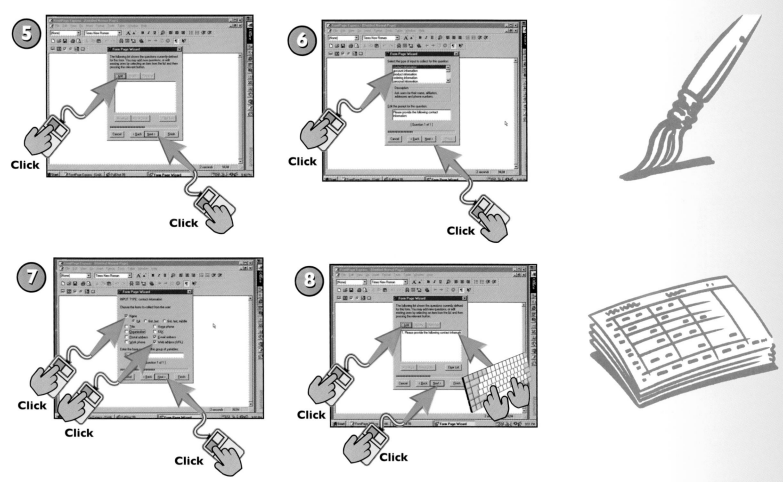

5   Click **Add** and then click **Next**.

6   Click **Contact Information** and then click **Next**.

7   Check to select or clear the check boxes for the types of contact information you want the form to collect and then click **Next**.

8   To add additional questions, click **Add** and type your question in the text box, or to accept the default question, click **Next**.

Creating an Interactive Form Continued

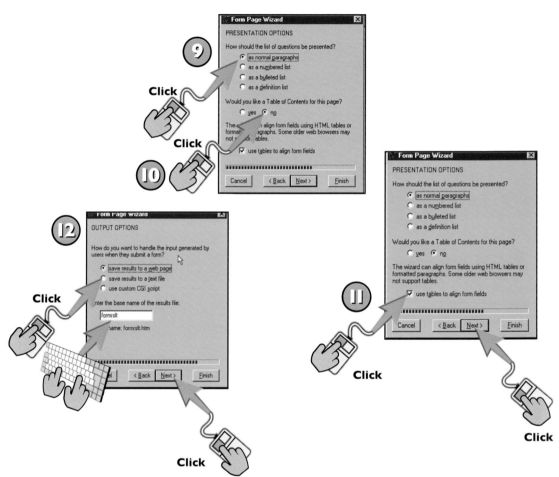

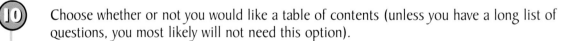

9 Choose how you want the list of questions displayed on the Web page by selecting the appropriate choices.

10 Choose whether or not you would like a table of contents (unless you have a long list of questions, you most likely will not need this option).

11 Select whether or not to use tables to align your form fields. It doesn't hurt to use this option—it makes your form fields more presentable) and click **Next**.

12 Choose how you want the form to submit the form information, enter the form name (or accept the default name), and click **Next**.

Next Step

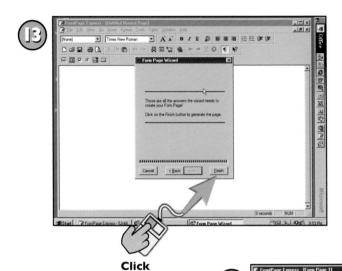

Click

✓ Changing Your Form's Appearance
You can edit the new page any way you like, such as formatting, adding text or pictures, and more. Just be careful not to delete the form fields.

✓ Exploring Different Form Types
This task demonstrated only one of the many different types of forms you can create by making different choices in the Form Page Wizard. Feel free to experiment.

13 Click **Finish**.

14 Make any additional changes to your form and be sure to save it.

Publishing Your Page Online

A play is not just lines on a page. Even after it is written and published, it does not officially become a play until an audience sees it on stage.

The same philosophy applies to a Web site. Even though you have created it, a Web site does not become real until it is published on the Internet. In this part, you find places on the Internet you can copy or upload your pages to the Web and more.

Tasks

Task #   Page #

1   Finding Space on a Web Server   110
2   Learning More About the Server You've Chosen   112
3   Getting Ready to Publish   113
4   Running the Web Publishing Wizard   114
5   Updating and Editing Your Page   118
6   Viewing Your Page Through the Internet   119
7   Getting Multiple Browser Programs for Testing   120
8   Getting Your Own Domain   122

Task 1: Finding Space on a Web Server

To be seen through the Web, your pages must be stored on a Web server. So, your first step is finding some Web server space to put your pages. It's likely you can get some space free from the *Internet service provider* (ISP, the company you pay for Internet access) or online server (such as America Online) you use. But, if you can't get free space there, you have other options to explore, which are described here in decreasing order of desirability.

 Determining Needed Server Space

How much server space do you need? Well, a single Web page file with text and a few pictures is usually smaller than 100 kilobytes (about 1/10th of a megabyte). So even a Web site made up of 10 or 12 different pages might fit in less than a megabyte of server space, unless your site includes a plethora of pictures or large media files, such as video clips.

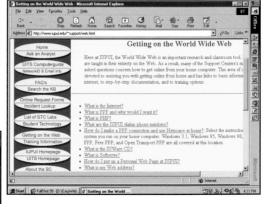

Call the Internet service provider (ISP) or the online service you use (or check out your service's Web page), and ask whether you can use some space on that company's Web server.

If the company you work for or the school you attend has its own Web site, they might let you use some space, particularly if your page is work or school related.

Go to Yahoo! (**www.yahoo.com**) or your favorite Web search tool, and enter **free Web space** as a search term. The search results will include companies offering free space.

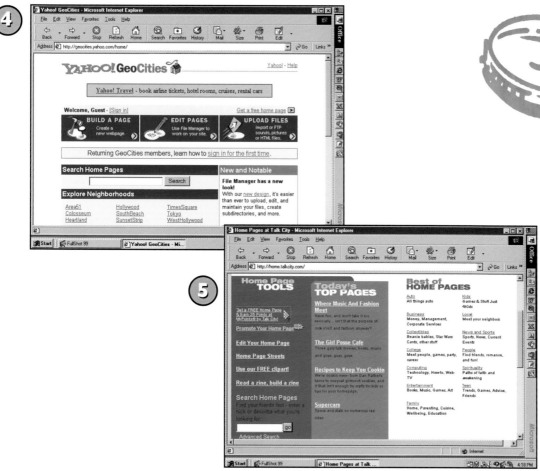

4. GeoCities is a company that offers free server space in exchange for the right to put advertising on your pages. Check out **www.geocities.com**.

5. Talk City is a fairly new service offering the same basic deal as GeoCities, but a different selection of tools for doing it. Explore **www.talkcity.com**.

Adhering to Host Requirements

GeoCities and Talk City both require special steps for putting your page online. These requirements include insisting that you join the GeoCities or Talk City community first, that you include their ads on your pages, and that you follow some unusual procedures for publishing your page (different from those you learn in this book). If you want to use one of these services, explore their Web sites thoroughly to learn the rules for joining and publishing.

After you choose your server, you need to know some stuff about it before you can publish there. Your ISP might give you this info over the phone, but ISPs can be hard to talk to. It is sometimes better to get this information online, if it's available there.

 Rounding Up the Needed Info

The information you need for publishing includes: The **URL** of the server (for example, www.myserver.com), the name of the directory in which you will store your files (usually the same as your username on the service), a password for copying your files to the server (often the same one you use to connect to the Internet), and the address of the server to which you will copy files (it might be the same as the final URL, but it might be a different address beginning with the letters **ftp**).

Task 2: Learning More About the Server You've Chosen

 Start Here

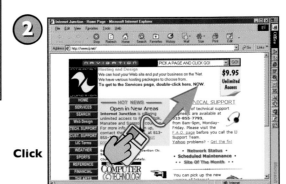

Click

Click

Go to the Web home page of the ISP, online service, or other organization from which you will get server space.

Look for links to User Homepages, Uploading Files, or other links that appear to lead to information about publishing your pages.

When you locate the information, click **File**, and then choose **Print** to print the information so you can refer to it while publishing your pages.

End Task

Task 3: Getting Ready to Publish

Start Here

①

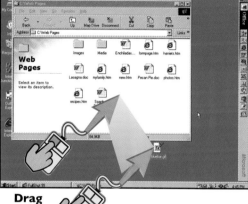
②

Drag

Drop

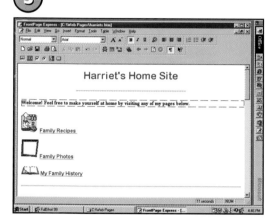
③

Publishing is usually pretty easy. However, problems have been known to occur. Most publishing problems happen not because publishing is difficult, but because the author failed to put his or her ducks in a row before starting the publishing steps. Here's how to get those ducks lined up smartly.

① Check that all the files making up your page or pages—HTML files, images, and any other files your page delivers through links—are all stored in the same folder.

② Delete or move from the folder anything that is not a part of the Web site, including any stray files or other folders.

③ Open your page and give it a final once-over, checking style, spelling, and links to bookmarks and files.

End Task

Task 4: Running the Web Publishing Wizard

Most server providers prefer that you upload—copy your Web files from your PC to the Web server—using an Internet tool called *FTP*. If you're familiar with FTP, you can do it that way. But Microsoft's Web Publishing Wizard—which is installed automatically when FrontPage Express is installed—can automatically publish via FTP, and in a few other ways, too. So if you don't already know FTP, there's no need to learn now—at least for publishing purposes.

✓ Closing Your Web Browser to Publish

If your Internet setup permits you to connect to the Internet without opening your Web browser, or to close your Web browser without disconnecting from the Internet, do that when you connect for this task. You don't need your Web browser while publishing your files, just your Internet connection.

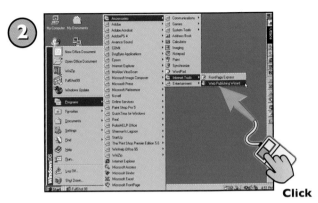

Click

Click

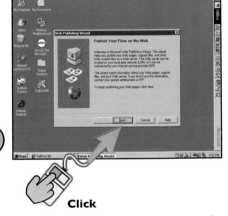

Click

1. Close FrontPage Express and any other programs you might have open, and connect to the Internet.

2. Click **Start**, click **Programs**, choose **Internet Explorer**, and choose **Web Publishing Wizard**.

3. Click **Next**.

Next Step

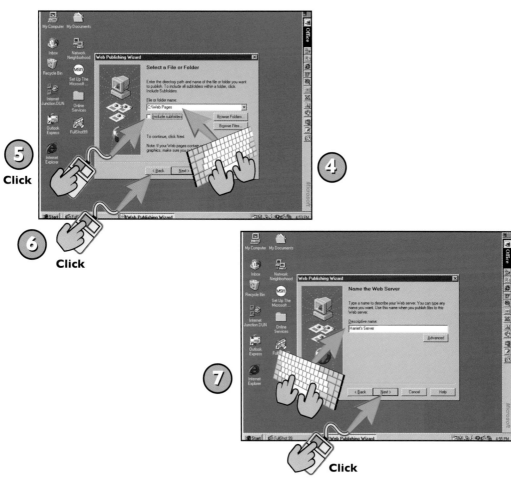

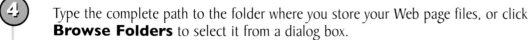

(4) Type the complete path to the folder where you store your Web page files, or click **Browse Folders** to select it from a dialog box.

(5) If a check mark appears in the **Include Subfolders** box, click to deselect it.

(6) Click **Next**.

(7) Type the server name and click **Next**.

Updating Your Site
If you want to publish a single file (such as an HTML file you've updated since you last published, see Task 5), add the filename to the end of the path in step 5. Only the file will be published—not all files in the folder.

Running Web Publishing Wizard Continued

Click

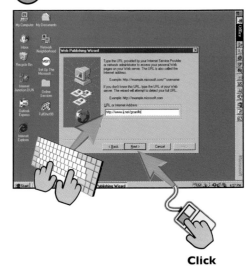

Click

**Providing a Web Address**

The URL you type in step 9 is the URL your visitors will use to visit your pages on the Web. To access your index.html file, they need only enter the URL exactly as shown in step 9. To access a Web file (other than index.html), they enter the URL, a slash (/), and then the filename; for example, **www.ij.net/gcarrillo/ harriets.html.**

8 In the upper box, type the complete **URL** of the server and directory in which your page will be published, and then click **Next**.

9 Type the URL of your Web site and click **Next**.

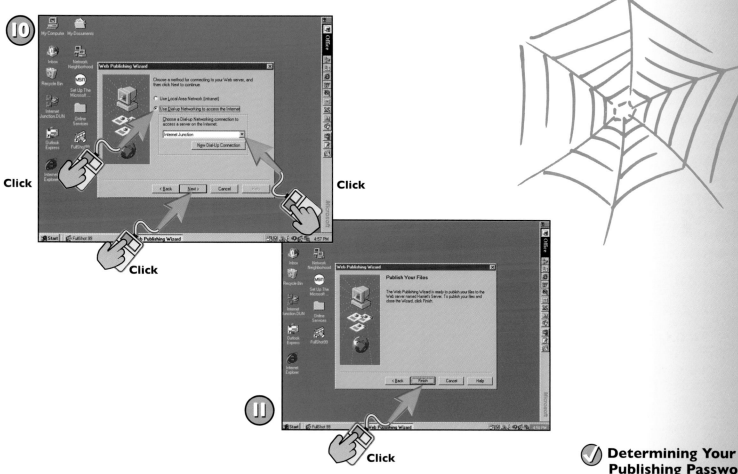

Click

Click

Click

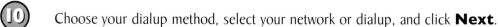

Click

10   Choose your dialup method, select your network or dialup, and click **Next**.

11   Click **Finish**. Wait while the Wizard uploads your pages to the server and then click **OK**.

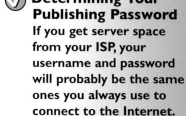

Determining Your Publishing Password
If you get server space from your ISP, your username and password will probably be the same ones you always use to connect to the Internet.

Task 5: Updating and Editing Your Page

If you find that you need to fix or update something on a page that you have already published, it is not a problem. You can't edit the copies of your pages stored on the Web server; instead, you simply make changes to the original files on your PC, and publish only those pages you changed. The changed files automatically replace the old ones on the server.

Click

Click

Click

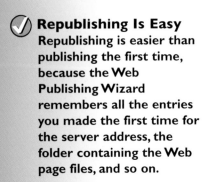

Republishing Is Easy
Republishing is easier than publishing the first time, because the Web Publishing Wizard remembers all the entries you made the first time for the server address, the folder containing the Web page files, and so on.

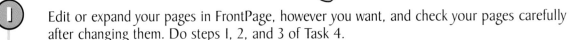

Edit or expand your pages in FrontPage, however you want, and check your pages carefully after changing them. Do steps 1, 2, and 3 of Task 4.

Click **Browse Files**, locate and select the file you changed, and click **Next**.

Complete the remainder of the wizard, just as you did in Task 4, and on the final dialog box, click **Finish**.

End
Task

Task 6: Viewing Your Page Through the Internet

Start Here

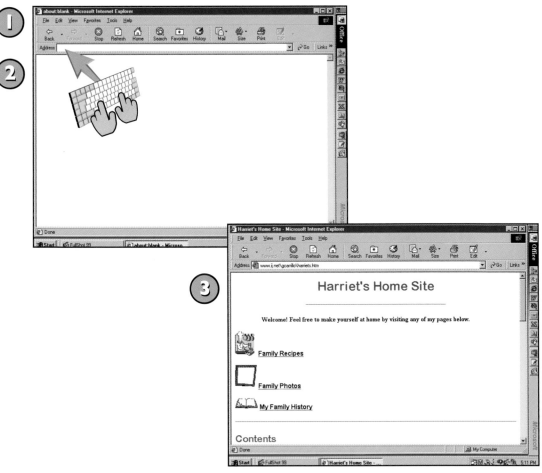

After you publish, you must test your Web pages through the Web, viewing it exactly as your visitors will. Besides, it's fun to see it online.

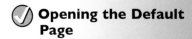
Opening the Default Page
If you named your top page **index.html** (as suggested in Part 2), that page opens automatically when a visitor surfs to the server directory without specifying a filename. For example, if the user enters the URL **www.server.com/harriet/** in his browser, the index.html file in the harriet directory opens automatically.

① Open your Web browser and connect to the Internet.

② In the **Address** box, type the Web page URL for your new page (including the filename of the HTML file you want to view), and press **Enter**.

③ Explore your page, evaluating its appearance and testing all your links. If you find any mistakes or anything else you want to change, refer to Task 5.

Task 7: Getting Multiple Browser Programs for Testing

So your page looks great in FrontPage Express and in your own Web browser. But that does not necessarily mean it will look great to everyone. There are subtle differences between browsers and those differences can make a page that looks great in one browser not look so great in another.

✓ **Seeking Help**
To download programs from the Internet and install them, see Part 10.

✓ **Ensuring Browser Compatibility**
If your page looks good in FrontPage Express, you can rest assured it will probably look fine in either Netscape Navigator or Internet Explorer, which means it will look fine to the majority of folks online. Still, there are small, subtle differences between even the most recent versions of these programs, so it's still smart to test in both and adjust your files as necessary.

Start Here

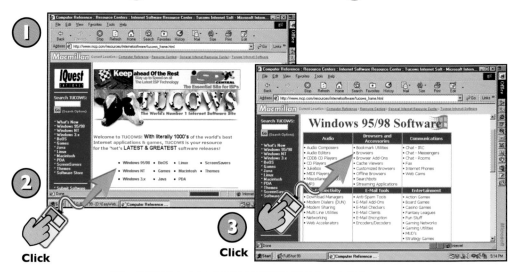

Click

Click

1 You can find browser programs lots of places online, but a good place to start is **tucows.mcp.com**.

2 Click the button for your system: **Win 95/98** or **Win NT**.

3 In the Browsers and Accessories box, click **Browsers**.

4 Scroll through the list, and use the links provided to learn about and download a variety of browsers you don't already have.

Next Step

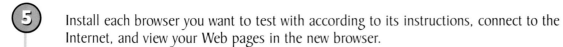

Testing Pages Offline
If you can figure out how to open *local files* (Web pages stored on your hard disk) in a particular browser, which can sometimes tricky, you can test pages offline by opening the Web files from your hard disk in your browser.

Changing Your Default Browser
When you install some browsers, they might try to make themselves your *default browser*—the one that opens automatically when you open a Web page file (refer to Part 2). If an unwanted browser makes itself the default, you can usually restore your original browser to its "default" status by reinstalling it.

5 Install each browser you want to test with according to its instructions, connect to the Internet, and view your Web pages in the new browser.

6 Use the browser to surf to your page and evaluate the page's appearance.

7 If you see major flaws that would make the page impossible to read, adjust the page in FrontPage Express, retest it in the new browser offline, and then republish it.

Task 8: Getting Your Own Domain

If you simply take some space on someone else's server, your page will be accessible through the Web, but it won't have the sort of catchy Web address that gives you a Web identity, such as www.buick.com. Instead, your page's address is expressed as a directory on the server; for example, www.servername.com/ harriet/. If you want to have your own Internet name—and have the cash— a domain is the way to go.

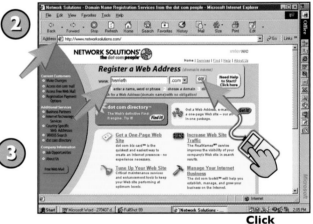

Click

✓ Mastering Your Domain

When typing your proposed domain in step 3, don't precede it with the "http://" or the "www" part, nor the ".com" at the end of the proposed address. These parts of the address are typical Web address parts, but not really part of the domain. For example, if you want your Web site address to be http://www.wild .com, just type wild in step 3.

 Think about what you want your Internet domain to be—for example, www.harriet.com.

 Visit the Network Solutions Web site—the official organization that registers Internet domains, at www.networksolutions.com.

3 In the **Search** box at the top of the page, type the domain you chose in step 1, and click **Go**.

Next Step

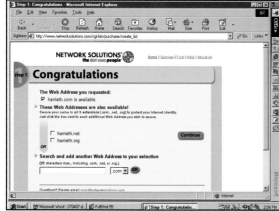

If Network Solutions displays a report that your proposed address is available, proceed to step 5. If your proposed address is already taken, return to step 1 and try a different name.

You can ask your ISP to register a domain for you or find another service by searching for **domain registration service**.

✓ Paying for Your Own Domain Name

Most ISPs will register a domain for around $50. In addition to the setup fee, the ISP will collect an additional $70 from you to pay a required registration fee to **Network Solutions**. That pays for your domain for two years; after that, you must pay **Network Solutions $35** per year to keep the domain.

✓ Choosing the Domain Type

The final part of the domain name can be **.com** (commercial site, the most common), **.org** (nonprofit organization, such as a foundation), **.edu** (educational institution), or **.net** (network). You'll be given a choice of which ones are available.

✓ Registering a Domain Yourself

You can register your domain yourself, if you know how, (saving the ISP's setup fee, but not the $70 due to Network Solutions) by filling in the forms provided on Network Solutions' Web site.

8

Announcing Your Page

After you have published your site to the Web, you need to get the word out on the street that you are open for business.

Of course, the scale of your Web site promotion efforts should match the ambitions of your page. If your page is just a personal home page for family, friends, and the occasional passing stranger, using just a couple of these methods—such as announcing by email—will suffice. Most people who publish Web sites do so because they **want** to be found by as many Web visitors as might have an interest in the site. This part shows you ways that help you get noticed.

Tasks

Task #		Page #
1	Finding Places to Promote Your Site	126
2	Listing Your Page in the Yahoo! Directory	128
3	Listing Your Page in the Excite Directory	130
4	Checking Out the Site Submission Services	131
5	Adding Your Web Address to Ads, Letterhead, and More	132
6	Announcing Your Page by Email	133

Task 1: Finding Places to Promote Your Site

Before beginning to promote your site, you should do a little surfing to locate the pages where you might want your page featured. Certainly the list includes the major search engines such as Yahoo!, Excite, and AltaVista, but it also includes smaller directory pages that feature links to pages covering the same topic as your site.

 Adding Your Site to a Search Engine

Most of the search engines have their own programs, called *crawlers* or *spiders*, that automatically search the Web and add new sites, using each site's title and contents to automatically determine which subject categories to list it in. But a few require you to manually add your site; you learn how to do this in Task 2.

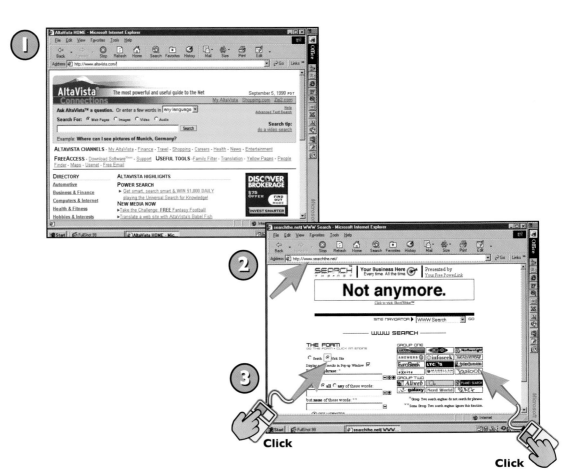

Click

Click

(1) Visit each of the major search tools, and look for links to information about adding or suggesting a new site.

(2) You can gain one-stop shopping to all the major search pages by going to **www.searchthe.net**.

(3) Click the **Visit Site** option button, and then click the search engine button you want to visit.

For any topic your page is related to, do a search to find pages covering that topic.

Some of those pages will include directories of links to related sites.

Send email to the Webmaster of sites containing directories, asking to have your site added to the list.

✓ **Ensuring Your Page Gets Listed**

The search tools with crawlers will find your page within a few weeks after you publish it. But the pages containing subject-specific directories rarely have crawlers; if you want to get listed there, you need to contact the Webmaster.

End Task

Yahoo! is the most popular directory on the Web. It's also one that does not catalog the Web automatically—you must add your site to Yahoo! to ensure that searchers find your site when doing a Yahoo! search on a term that's related to your site's contents.

✓ **Choosing a Yahoo! Category**
If the category you choose in step 2 is too broad, Yahoo! will display a message to that effect, and ask you to choose another, more specific category before proceeding.

Task 2: Listing Your Page in the Yahoo! Directory

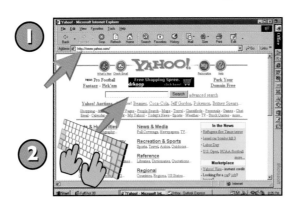

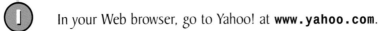

In your Web browser, go to Yahoo! at **www.yahoo.com**.

Use Yahoo!'s search box, or browse through its category listings, to go to a category in which your site belongs.

Scroll to the bottom of the page on which your selected category list appears, and click **Suggest a Site**.

Read the Suggest a Site page for tips on properly listing your page with Yahoo!.

Next Step

Click

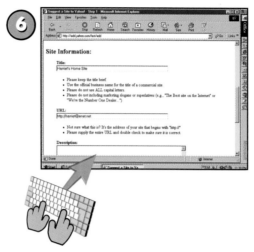

Click

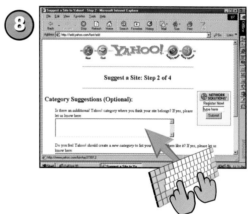

⑤ Scroll to the bottom of the Suggest a Site page, and click **Proceed to Step One**.

⑥ Scroll down to the Site Information form, and type the title and URL of your page or site, plus a brief description.

⑦ At the bottom of the Suggest a Site page, click **Proceed to Step Two**.

⑧ Continue through steps 2, 3, and 4, filling in all information requested and clicking the button at the bottom of the page to proceed to each new step.

Describing Your Page to Yahoo! Users
The description you type in step 6 will appear in the search results whenever someone's Yahoo! search finds your page. Word it carefully, to help searchers determine whether your page contains what they want. Be sure, also, to include in the description keywords that are related to the page's topic.

End Task

Listing your page on Excite is much simpler than doing so in Yahoo! Excite uses a program to search through each site's pages, using the page's contents to determine which categories to list it in. So all you have to do is let Excite know where your site is—the program does the rest.

Task 3: Listing Your Page in the Excite Directory

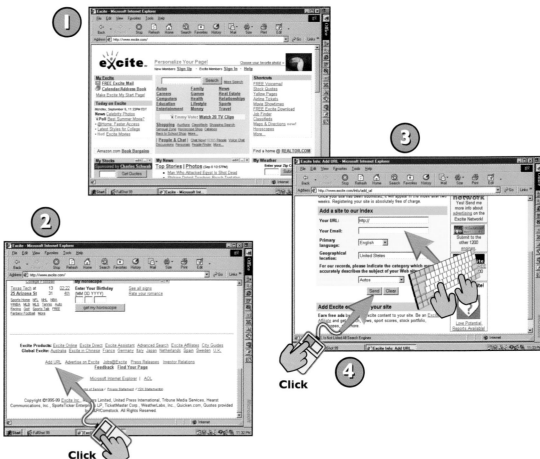

Start Here

Click

Click

Waiting for Your Site to Appear

After you manually add your site to Yahoo! or Excite, it probably won't show up right away. Typically, it takes about two weeks for your site to show up in the listings.

① In your Web browser, go to Excite at **www.excite.com**.

② Scroll to the bottom of the page, and click **Add URL**.

③ Fill in the **Your URL** of your page (or top page of your site) and **Your Email** address, so Excite can contact you if necessary.

④ Click **Send**.

End Task

Task 4: Checking Out the Site Submission Services

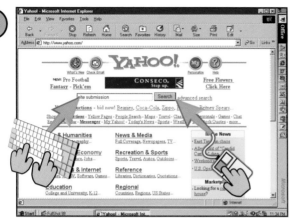

Click

You can promote your site effectively by simply adding it to Yahoo! and the directories on a few related pages, and then waiting for the crawlers to get you listed in most other search tools. Also, there are commercial site submission services. They submit your site to all the major search tools, plus hundreds of other directories. The fee for the service ranges from under $10 to more than $100.

1 In the box at the top of the main Yahoo! page (**www.yahoo.com**), type **site submission** and click **Search**.

2 In the search results, read the descriptions to find sites that offer site submission.

3 Visit the sites to learn what the service offers (and what it costs).

✓ **Submitting Your Site with Software**
There are also site-submission software packages you install on your **PC**. Check out a product called **Submissions** at **www.submissions.com**.

Task 5: Adding Your Web Address to Ads, Letterhead, and More

Some of the best places to publicize your page are not online, but off. All those big companies put their Web site addresses on billboards, in newspaper ads, and in TV commercials for a reason. You can advertise your site in your own way too.

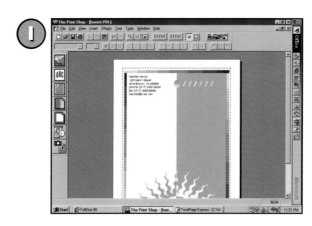

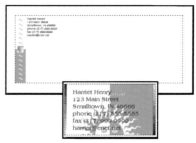

Making Your Address More Visible

Wherever you can do so without disrupting the design of your printed publications, print the URL in a bright, unique color to make it stand out—just the way it does online.

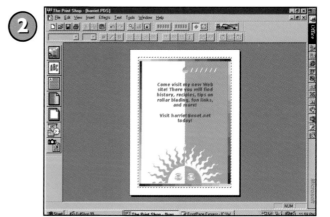

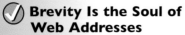

Brevity Is the Soul of Web Addresses

These days, it's not necessary to include the prefix "http://" when showing your URL in print. That's great, because leaving off the prefix makes the URL look shorter, less technical, and easier to remember.

 Add your Web site address to your stationery, business cards, business or personal newsletter, and advertising.

2 For a business or personal site, put out a special flier announcing your Web site.

Task 6: Announcing Your Page by Email

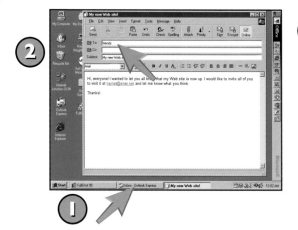

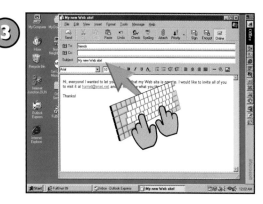

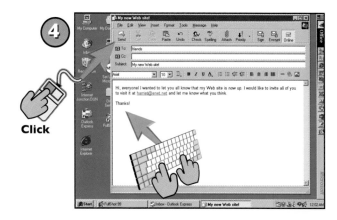

Click

Of course, the best source of visitors for your Web page is the pool of people already online. You can reach them most effectively using email. An email announcement to friends, clients, or customers is a great way to inaugurate a new Web site.

✓ **Sending Links Via Email**

After you type the URL, most email programs automatically create a link out of the URL you typed. This way the recipients of your email can just click the link and go straight to your site.

✓ **Adding Pizzazz to Your Email**

Email is letterhead, too. People with their own Web sites add a note at the bottom of all their email correspondence—an *email signature*—listing their Web site address. Outlook Express and other email clients let you create such a signature; consult your program's Help file or documentation to learn how to do so.

1 In Outlook Express (Internet Explorer 4's email program) or other any other email program, type an announcement message.

2 Address the message to recipients. Use a distribution list or type each email address in the **To:** line, separating each with semicolons (**;**).

3 Enter a meaningful and enticing **Subject** line.

4 Type your message and don't forget to include your URL. Click **Send** to transmit it.

End Task

Super Editing: HTML

OK, so you have created HTML files by writing the HTML code yourself. And, that's what FrontPage Express created, behind the scenes, each time you created a page. HTML is the code that all Web authoring programs create.

The HTML file itself is just an ordinary tag language that uses the filename extension .htm or .html to identify and distinguish it from other languages. Inside the file, you find the text of your page and its title, plus an array of little codes, called *tags*. The tags are what makes HTML work. When a browser opens an HTML file, it reads and obeys the tags, which tell the browser what each object is (a heading, a paragraph, a link), the filenames and positions of any pictures, the URLs the links point to, and so on.

Actually, Web authoring programs are so easy to use that you could perceivably continue to progress as a Web author and never actually touch raw HTML. However, even with an *Easy* introduction to Web authoring, it's a good idea to at least explore the basics of HTML.

Tasks

Task #		Page #
1	What Is HTML, Exactly?	136
2	Creating a Web Page in HTML	138
3	Adding a Picture Through HTML	142
4	Applying Formatting to Text	144
5	Learning How to Use All the HTML Tags	145

Task 1: What Is HTML, Exactly?

A good way to begin understanding HTML is to explore the HTML file of your own Web page. That way, you can often guess what many of the tags are doing, because you created it yourself, which will give you a good idea of how the HTML tags do their thing.

Click

Color My World
In its HTML view, FrontPage Express color-codes the HTML tags to help authors see them. But the color-coding doesn't really mean anything, and when you create your own HTML tags, you certainly don't have to worry what color they are!

1 In FrontPage Express, open a simple page you've created.

2 Click **View**, and then choose **HTML** to see the raw HTML code of the page.

Next Step

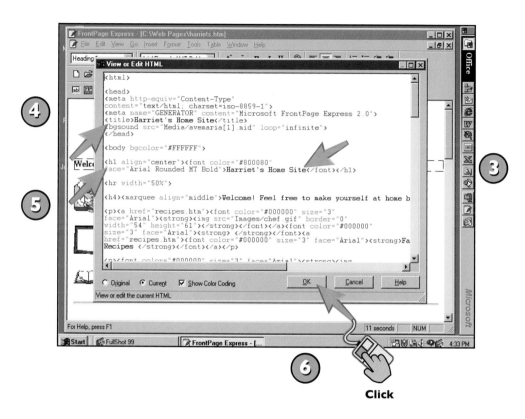

Click

3 Examine the page, ignoring the tags and looking for content you put there: your words, the filenames of pictures, the URLs of your links.

4 Now look at all the HTML tags, which are enclosed in carats (**< >**).

5 Observe that you can tell on sight what some tags do. For example, before text to which you've applied a level-1 Heading paragraph style, you'll see the tag <h1>—Heading 1.

6 Click **OK** to return to the regular FrontPage Express view.

Pairing Up
If you look closely at the tags, you'll notice that most (but not all) work in pairs. For example, somewhere near the top of the file, you'll see the tag <title>, followed by your page's title, followed by another tag, </title>. That's how tags usually work; one tag marks the start of something, and another tag (the same, only with the added slash at the front) marks the end.

End Task

Most of the job of creating a Web page in HTML involves typing tags and content. But first you need to understand the big picture, the way an HTML file must be organized into two sections: the header (which contains the page title, and sometimes other, optional stuff), and the body (the part of the file where you define everything you see in the page layout). Because an HTML file is just a text file, you can create it in any text editor, such as Windows's Notepad accessory.

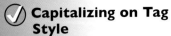

Capitalizing on Tag Style

When you type HTML tags, it doesn't matter whether you use uppercase letters (<H1>) or lowercase letters (<h1>). Some Web authors prefer using capital letters, because doing so makes it easier to see the tags buried within the text of the page. However, you can use either case.

Task 2: Creating a Web Page in HTML

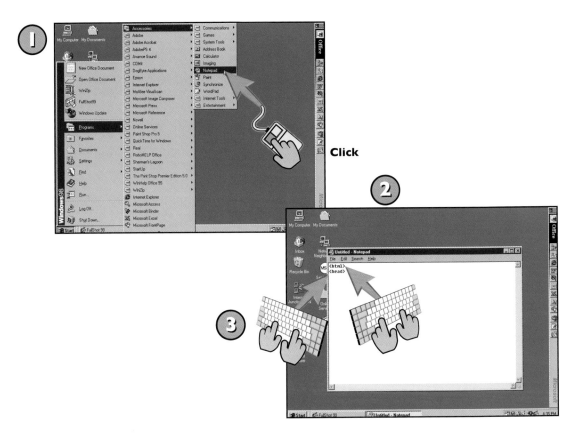

Click

1. Click **Start**, then **Programs**, then **Accessories**, and then **Notepad**.

2. Type **<html>**, to mark the start of the file, and press **Enter** to start a new line.

3. Type **<head>** to start the header, and then press **Enter**.

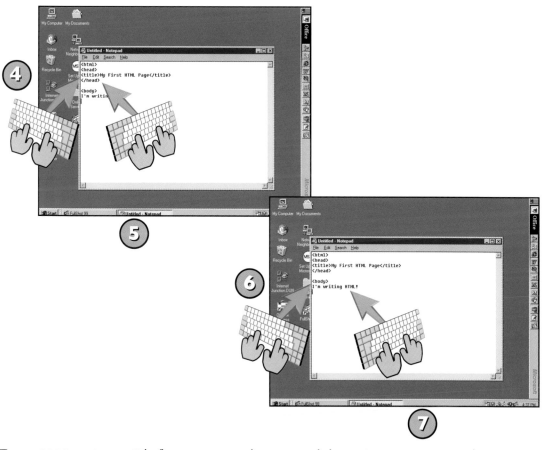

Using HTML in Addition to FrontPage Express
FrontPage Express does a lot for you, but it does not give you toolbar buttons or menu items for absolutely everything that can be done in HTML. That's why working in HTML is important. You can still save time by working primarily in FrontPage Express or another WYSIWYG (what you see is what you get) editor, then edit the HTML code directly to add tags your WYSIWYG editor does not supply.

(4) Type **\<title\>**, type a title for your page, close your tab by typing **\</title\>**, and press **Enter**.

(5) Type \</head\> to mark the end of the header and press **Enter**.

(6) Type \<body\> to mark the start of the body of text and press **Enter**.

(7) Type **I'm writing HTML!** and press **Enter**.

Creating a Web Page in HTML Continued

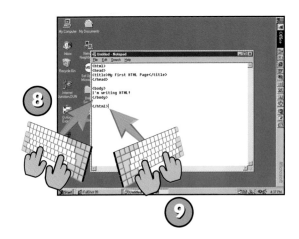

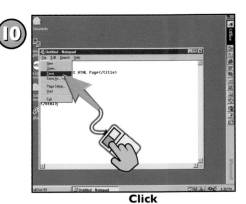

Click

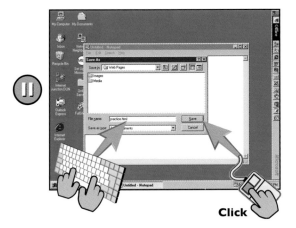

Click

Next Step

✓ Catching the Code

Most browsers let you view the raw HTML code, called *source code*, of pages you're viewing. This enables you to learn about HTML by studying the pages you visit online. While viewing a page in Internet Explorer 5, choose **View** and then **Source**. In Navigator, choose **View** and then **Page Source**.

8 Type **</body>** to mark the end of the body.

9 Type **</html>** to mark the end of the file.

10 Click **File**, and then choose **Save**.

11 Choose a folder (or the desktop) to store the file in, type **practice.html** for the filename, and then click the **Save** button.

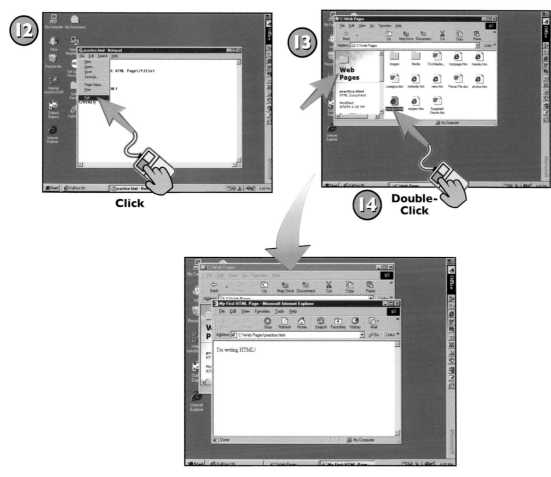

Click

Double-Click

Error-Checking Your Code

If you don't see what you should when you view the HTML file through a browser, it's usually because of a minor HTML coding error. If you forget to create both a header and body, or forget to use close tags (the ones with the slash in them, such as </body>), or misspell a tag, the browser cannot render or display the file correctly. If this happens, go back and check your tags carefully.

Viewing Code with Notepad

When you choose **File, Open** in Notepad to reopen an HTML file you're working on, you won't see the HTML file in Notepad's Open dialog box, even after you navigate to the right folder. At first, that box shows only files ending in **.txt**. Open the list at the bottom of the Open dialog box, and choose **All Files (*.*)**. Then your HTML file will appear in the box so you can select and open it.

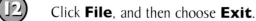

Click **File**, and then choose **Exit**.

In Windows, open the folder where you stored **practice.html**.

Double-click the icon to display the file in your default browser.

End Task

Task 3: Adding a Picture Through HTML

After you have the header and body set up in your HTML file, you can begin adding tags and content. To get a taste of how tags work, add a picture to your basic HTML file. Just for practice, use FrontPage Express's built-in HTML source editor to add the tag.

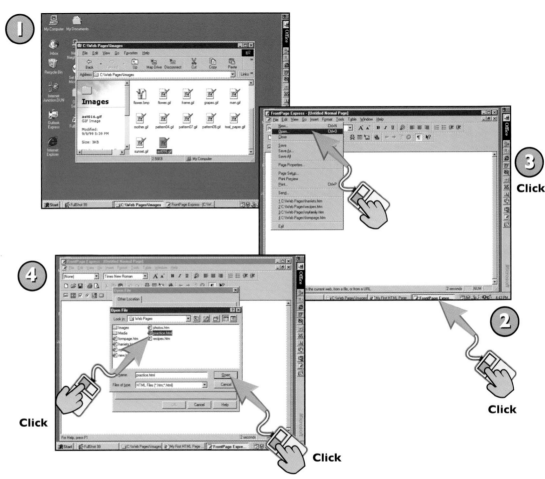

Click

Click

Click

Click

Click

Click

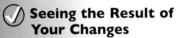

✓ **Seeing the Result of Your Changes**
To play with HTML, you can open this HTML view, make changes to the HTML codes or anything else on the page, and then click **OK** to return to FrontPage Express and see the results of your changes in FrontPage Express's regular "browser" view of the file.

(1) Prepare an image file, and store it in the same folder as the practice.html file you created in Task 2.

(2) Open FrontPage Express.

(3) Click **File**, and then choose **Open**.

(4) Click **Browse**, navigate to the folder (or desktop) where practice.html is stored, click **practice.html**, and click **Open**.

Next Step

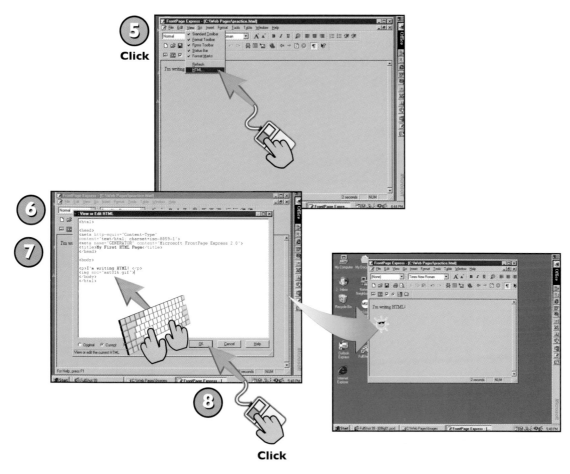

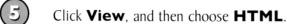

Click

✓ Seeing Changes FrontPage Express Makes

When you create a file in Notepad or another text editor, then view its source through FrontPage Express, you'll notice tags you never wrote, and other minor changes. FrontPage automatically adds some optional tags and deletes unnecessary (but harmless) line breaks in the HTML coding.

✓ Undoing HTML Coding

If, when you view the page back in FrontPage Express view, you don't like the results of the last HTML change you made, you can undo it by clicking **Edit**, and then choosing **Undo**.

---

⑤ Click **View**, and then choose **HTML**.

⑥ In the body, between your line of text and the closing body tag, type **<IMG SRC=** (the start of the HTML tag that inserts an image in a page).

⑦ Follow the equals sign (=) with a quote mark ("), the filename of the image file, another quote mark ("), and a close carat (>).

⑧ Click **OK** to close the HTML editor and view the page in FrontPage Express.

Task 4: Applying Formatting to Text

The tag that adds images is a little unusual, in that it doesn't work in pairs like most tags. To get a better sense of how tags usually work, add tags to apply level-1 heading format, center the heading on the page, and make a word within the heading *italic*.

✓ **Aligning Your Alignment Codes**
Observe the fact that the *align* tag goes *inside* the **<h1>** tag. Some special tags, called *attributes*, go inside other tags to modify the for-matting applied by the main tag. The align attributes (center, left, right) go inside the tags for a paragraph (**<p>**), heading (**<h1>, <h2>**...), and image (**<img src**...) to align those objects.

✓ **Starting New Paragraphs**
To add more paragraphs to your sample file, simply pressing **Enter** to start a new line doesn't work. You must start each new paragraph with one of the heading tags (**<h1>**) or with a new paragraph tag (**<p>**).

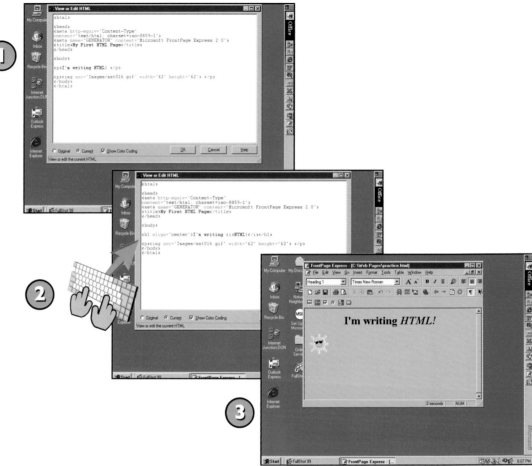

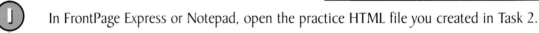

In FrontPage Express or Notepad, open the practice HTML file you created in Task 2.

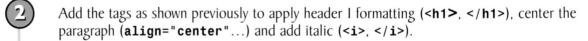

Add the tags as shown previously to apply header 1 formatting (**<h1>**, **</h1>**), center the paragraph (**align="center"**...) and add italic (**<i>**, **</i>**).

View the page in your browser or in FrontPage's regular view, to see the results.

Task 5: Learning How to Use All the HTML Tags

 Start Here

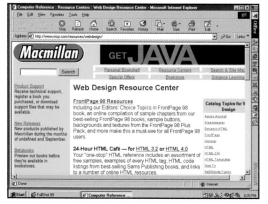

 Click

If you want to learn more about **HTML**, there are several good ways to get started. Not surprisingly, many of the best beginner's **HTML** primers and reference guides can be found online. *The 24-Hour HTML Café* is a good place to start.

✓ **Be Aware of Version Changes**
HTML changes from time to time, which is why you see choices for information about **HTML 3.2** and others for **HTML 4.0**. The older version usually contains 99% of the same tags as the newer version, and is more stable. So beginners are better off studying the older standard first, when a choice is offered.

✓ **Reading Further**
Dozens of books can tell you how to use all the **HTML** tags properly. The creator of the HTML Cafe, Dick Oliver, wrote *Teach Yourself HTML in 24 Hours*, which is a good choice for an author newly graduated from *Easy Web Page Publishing*.

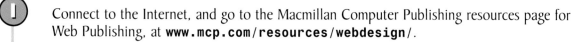

① Connect to the Internet, and go to the Macmillan Computer Publishing resources page for Web Publishing, at **www.mcp.com/resources/webdesign/**.

② Scroll down to the link for **24-Hour HTML Café** and click the link to **HTML 3.2**.

③ The 24-Hour HTML Café page opens.

End Task

PART 10

Discovering Other Web Authoring Tools and Techniques

With nothing more than FrontPage Express and the occasional bit of HTML editing, you can do most of what other Web authors do.

Before you leave this *Easy* book, it's important to know that there are other tools and utilities you can add to your Web authoring arsenal—especially now that you've developed a solid foundation through the tools you've learned.

In particular, there are other general-purpose Web authoring programs that can serve special needs or when you're ready to move up to more advanced tools. You'll learn a few such programs in this final part. I will also show you how to find other programs and resources online that will expand your Web-publishing prowess.

Tasks

Task #		Page #
1	Finding Authoring Programs on the Web	148
2	Learning About Microsoft FrontPage	150
3	Learning About Netscape Composer	151
4	Finding Graphics Utilities and Other Helpful Programs	152
5	Downloading Programs from the Web	154
6	Downloading WinZip	155
7	Learning About Advanced Authoring Techniques	156

Task 1: Finding Authoring Programs on the Web

There are many Web-authoring tools, including commercial, shareware, and freeware programs. New tools appear all the time. So being aware of the best-known tools (as you will be, after the next few tasks) isn't enough. To keep up with what's new and where to get it, you need to know how to search for the Web authoring tools available online. Here are a few ways to start.

Start Here

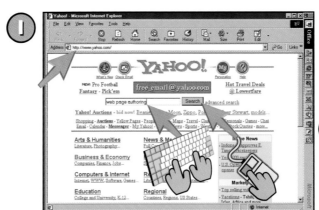

Click

✓ **Trying Other Search Terms**
Other good search terms to try in step 2 include **HTML editor, HTML authoring,** and **Web publishing.**

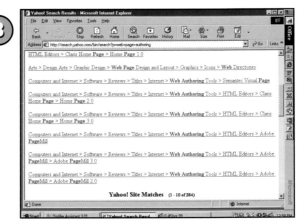

✓ **Giving Other Products a Trial Run**
When searching, pay particular attention to lesser-known, little tools, especially shareware products. Often these are more innovative than the popular tools you hear about the most.

① Go to the Yahoo! search page at **www.yahoo.com**.

② In the **Search** box, type **Web page authoring**, and then click **Search**.

③ The search results will show many categories and sites you can browse to find authoring programs and other Web authoring stuff.

Next Step

Click

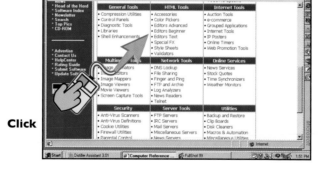

Click

④ You can also find plenty of tools by visiting the TUCOWS library at **tucows.mcp.com**.

⑤ Click the button for your system: **Windows 95/98** or **Windows NT**.

⑥ Look in the **HTML Tools** box for likely links, such as **Editors Beginner**, and click.

✅ **Adding Special Effects**
In the **HTML Tools** box on TUCOWS, notice the link for **Special FX**. This link leads to fun tools for adding animation, sound, and other pizzazz to your pages.

✅ **Seeing What's New**
Note the links in TUCOWS's far-left column. The What's New link offers a quick way to check for the latest tools.

✅ **Looking for Links**
If you want to try other search sites on your own, check out **CNET's builder.com**—it has some great links to explore, too.

End Task

Task 2: Learning About Microsoft FrontPage

On the one hand, Microsoft's FrontPage, big brother to FrontPage Express, is the logical next step up for someone who's already experienced with the junior Express version. Although FrontPage offers you many powerful capabilities not included in Express, nearly everything you know how to do now is done the same way in FrontPage. So, it's an easy and logical step up. On the other hand, FrontPage isn't free. While trying to decide on your next move, visit the FrontPage Web site to learn more.

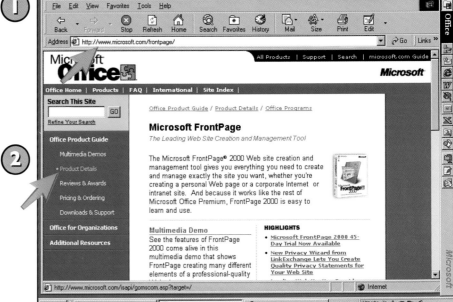

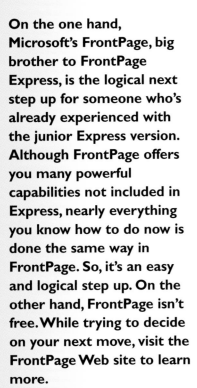

✓ Trying FrontPage for Free

Note that, at the writing of this book, Microsoft was offering a free 45-day trial of FrontPage using a link on the FrontPage Web site for a small fee ($6.95). When you visit, keep your eyes out for such offers, so you can try before you buy.

 Connect to the Internet, and point your browser to **www.microsoft.com/frontpage/**.

 Explore the links to learn more about FrontPage and how to get it.

Task 3: Learning About Netscape Composer

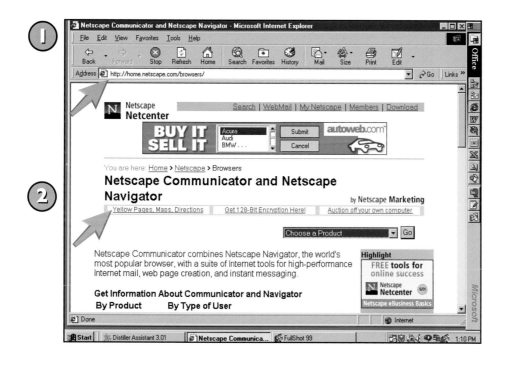

Just as FrontPage Express comes free with Internet Explorer 5, Composer, Netscape's Web authoring program, comes free with Communicator, Netscape's all-in-one Internet software package. Composer is very similar to FrontPage Express, but it does a few things Express doesn't. For example, it gives you better control of the positioning of pictures on a page. Those capabilities make Composer a nice companion to FrontPage Express.

Getting More Detail on Netscape Composer

The book *Teach Yourself to Create a Web Page in 24 Hours* is not only a good next book for someone who started with *Easy Web Pages*, but also one that shows in detail how to use Composer. The book includes Communicator (with Composer, of course) and other Web-authoring tools on its free CD-ROM.

1 Point your browser to **home.netscape.com/browsers/**.

2 Explore the links to learn more about Communicator and Composer.

Task 4: Finding Graphics Utilities and Other Helpful Programs

So far, you've already discovered several good online sources for programs, including **TUCOWS** (`tucows.mcp.com`). But **TUCOWS** alone doesn't offer the incredible range of programs and files available from Download.com—your first stop when you want to find and download graphics utilities and other useful Web-authoring accessories.

✓ **Finding Graphics Utilities and Web Authoring Tools**

Download.com and similar sites (such as **Shareware.com**) are great for finding smaller, accessory-type tools—such as graphics utilities—but not for big tools, such as your primary Web authoring program. For those, it's better to go to the home page for that tool (or use Yahoo! or another search tool to locate the home page) to get more detailed information about the program than Download.com supplies.

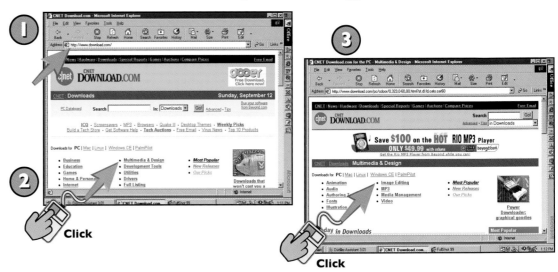

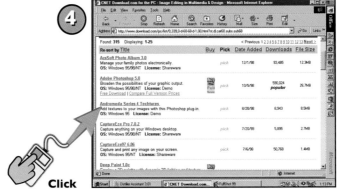

Go to Download.com at **www.download.com**.

Click the **Multimedia and Design** category.

Click **Image Editing**.

Scroll through the list of Image Editing programs and files, and click one that looks interesting.

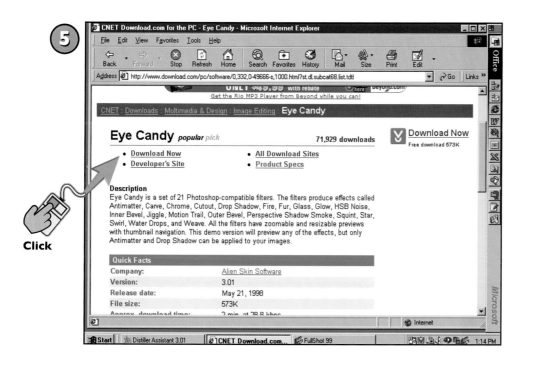

Click

(5) Read the description, and if you want the program, click the **Download Now** link.

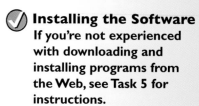

✓ Installing the Software
If you're not experienced with downloading and installing programs from the Web, see Task 5 for instructions.

If you've downloaded and installed programs from the Web before, you don't need this task. But because this book has shown a variety of great places to download programs, clip art, and more, it's only fair to cover the basics of downloading.

✓ Accessing Compressed Files

Often, the files and programs you download from the Web are *zipped*, compressed into an archive file so that they take up less space (and thus download faster). A zipped file uses the filename extension **.zip**, and its icon looks like a clamp around a file cabinet. Before you can use the contents of a zipped file, you might have to decompress it—*unzip* it—with a program such as WinZip (see Task 6). Other zipped files are *self-extracting*; that is, you just double-click the file's icon and the files decompress by themselves.

Task 5: Downloading Programs from the Web

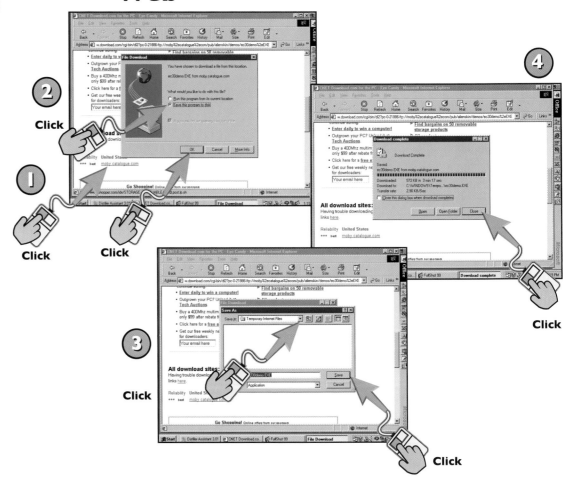

① Go online, navigate to the link for downloading the file, and click it to start the download.

② Choose **Save This Program to Disk**, and then click **OK**.

③ Use the **Save In** list to choose the folder in which to save the downloaded file. But don't change the filename. Then click **Save**.

④ The download begins. When the download is finished, a message appears to tell you so. Click **Close**.

Task 6: Downloading WinZip

Start
Here

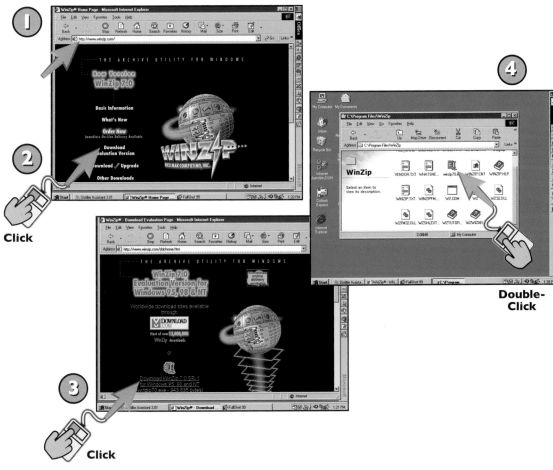

Click

Click

Double-Click

A shareware program, WinZip is just one of several programs available online for unzipping zipped files. You know you have downloaded a zipped file when the file's extension is .zip and its icon looks like a file cabinet caught in a clamp. After you have WinZip, you'll be equipped to handle the larger Windows programs and files available online.

✓ **Using WinZip to Extract Files**
After WinZip is installed, you can unzip files by double-clicking the file's icon, which opens the file in WinZip. In WinZip, you click the **Extract** button to unzip the open file.

✓ **Creating Archives with WinZip**
WinZip not only unzips, but also zips. You can use WinZip to zip up multiple files into a single archive file, which saves space wherever you store the file. Archiving is a great way to preserve your Web pages as they evolve.

① Go to www.winzip.com.

② Click the link labeled **Download Evaluation Version**.

③ Scroll down and click the link for the **Windows 95, 98 and NT** versions to begin the download.

④ After the download is complete, double-click the **WinZip** icon to install WinZip.

End
Task

Task 7: Learning About Advanced Authoring Techniques

So, what's on the horizon now? As a budding Web author, you're ready to begin exploring some not-so-*Easy* authoring techniques, such as Java and JavaScript (used for programming scripts that expand a Web page's capabilities beyond plain HTML), advanced multimedia, and more. For help, here are some good places to begin your next Web adventures. Another good site is Microsoft's MSDN Web Workshop at `msdn.microsoft.com`.

  Start Here

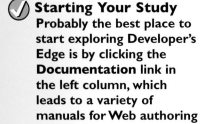 **Starting Your Study**
Probably the best place to start exploring Developer's Edge is by clicking the **Documentation** link in the left column, which leads to a variety of manuals for Web authoring techniques.

 For an extensive selection of tutorials, reference pages, and other advanced authoring resources, visit Netscape's Developer's Edge site at `developer.netscape.com`.

2 For a more modest and simple selection of authoring tips, go to the InformIT page at `www.informit.com/webedit`.

 Next Step

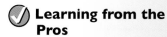

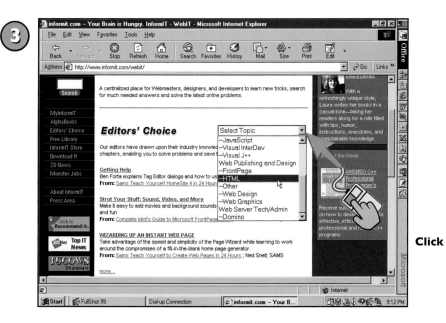

Click

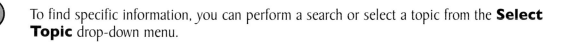

③ To find specific information, you can perform a search or select a topic from the **Select Topic** drop-down menu.

alignment   The way text is placed on a page. Left-aligned text lines up to the left margin, right-aligned text lines up to the right margin, and centered text is centered between the left and right margins.

animated GIF   A special kind of GIF (Graphics Interchange Format) image file that plays as a brief, animated clip when viewed through a browser.

background   A color or image that covers the entire area behind the text and pictures of a Web page.

bookmark   An invisible marker on a Web page that provides a spot to which a link can point, used to take a visitor straight to that specific spot on the page. Bookmarks are also known as **targets** or **anchors** in some Web authoring programs.

browse   To wander around the World Wide Web portion of the Internet, viewing Web pages through a browser. This is also known as **surfing** or **cruising** the Net.

browser   A program, such as Internet Explorer or Netscape Navigator, that enables you to view Web pages.

bulleted list   A list of items in which each item is preceded by a marker, a "bullet" or some other symbol character. **See also** numbered list.

CGI   Short for **Common Gateway Interface**. One method for creating interactive sites, such as those that use scripts to make advanced Web page features work, such as forms. **See also** Java, JavaScript.

character formatting   Formatting that changes the style of characters, such as applying fonts, bold, or italic.

check box   A small, square box used to select objects in a program or a Web page. Clicking an empty check box inserts a check mark there, indicating that the object or option next to the check box is selected.

close tag   An HTML tag required at the end of a block of code. For every beginning tag, there must be close tag. Close tags begin with **</**, for example, </bold>.

dialog box   A box that pops up in Windows programs to provide the options necessary for completing a particular task. Different tasks display different dialog boxes.

domain   The address of a computer on the Internet. A user's Internet address is made up of a username and a domain name. Every Web server has its own unique domain and can play host to other domains, as well.

download   The act of copying information from a server computer to your computer. **See also** upload.

email address   The Internet address an email program uses to send email to a specific Internet user. The address is typically made up of a username, an @ sign, and a domain name (**user@domain**).

FAQ file   Short for **Frequently Asked Questions file**. A computer file, often made available on the Internet, containing the answers to frequently asked questions about a particular topic or Web site.

font   A particular style of text.

form   A part of a Web page in which users can type entries or make selections that are then collected and processed.

freeware   Software available to anyone, free of charge (unlike shareware, which requires payment), often available for download from the Internet.

FrontPage Express   A Web page authoring program from Microsoft, included in the free Internet Explorer suite of Internet programs (for Windows 95 and NT) and also built into Windows 98.

FTP Short for *File Transfer Protocol*. The basic method for copying a file from one computer to another through the Internet, often used for publishing Web page files by uploading them to a server.

GIF Short for *Graphics Interchange Format*. A form of a bitmapped file format (image file), commonly used for inline images in Web pages.

heading A short line of text, often set large and bold, that marks the start of a specific section of a document, such as a Web page.

horizontal line In a Web page, a straight line that divides sections of the page horizontally. Sometimes known as a *horizontal rule*.

HTML Short for *Hypertext Markup Language*. The document formatting language used to create Web pages. The files produced by Web authoring programs like FrontPage Express are HTML files.

hyperlink *See* link.

inline image An image that appears within the layout of a Web page.

Internet A large, loosely organized internetwork connecting universities, research institutions, governments, businesses, and other organizations so that they can exchange messages and share information.

Internet Explorer A browser created by Microsoft, which is used to view Web pages. Internet Explorer version 5 is built into Windows 98, and is available free for other systems (Windows 95 and NT, Macintosh, and UNIX). Most versions of Internet Explorer 5 include FrontPage Express.

intranet An internal, corporate network, usually a local area network, that is based on Internet technologies. It is used just like the World Wide Web— through a browser.

Java, JavaScript Two different methods for creating scripts, used for some advanced Web page features, such as interactive forms. *See also* CGI.

JPEG Short for *Joint Photographic Experts Group*. A form of an image file, usually photographic pictures, commonly used for inline images in Web pages.

link Short for *hyperlink*, an object on a Web page that takes the visitor to another page, downloads a file, or starts some other action.

link source The part of a link that a visitor actually sees on a Web page and clicks to activate the link. (The other part of a link is the URL.) A link source can be text or a picture.

list box In a dialog box or Web page, a small box with a downward-pointing arrow on the right. Clicking the arrow opens a list of options the user can click to select.

mailto link A link in a Web page that, when clicked by a visitor, opens the visitor's email program and creates a new message, preaddressed to a particular person.

marquee A line of text that repeatedly scrolls across part of a Web page, used as an attention-getting device.

menu A list of choices on a computer screen. A user selects one choice to perform an action with a software program.

Mosaic A browser, available as freeware.

Navigator Sometimes called Netscape, a popular browser from Netscape Communications. Navigator is available in a suite, called Netscape Communicator, which also includes programs for Web authoring, email, and other tools.

netiquette   The code of proper conduct (etiquette) on the Internet or the Net.

Netscape   Short for **Netscape Communications**, a software company that developed and markets Navigator. Some people casually refer to Navigator and Communicator as "Netscape."

network   A set of computers interconnected so that they can communicate and share information. Connected networks together form an internetwork.

Notepad   A program included with all versions of Windows which allows the user to view, edit, and print plain text files, such as HTML files.

numbered list   A list of items in which each item is preceded by a number, and the numbers go up as the list goes down. **See also** bulleted list.

paragraph formatting   Text formatting, such as paragraph styles or alignment, that can be applied only to a whole paragraph or paragraphs, never to only selected characters within a paragraph, like character formatting.

paragraph style   The principal form of text formatting on a Web page. Paragraph styles include six levels of headings, a style for normal text, and several different styles for creating lists.

search engine   A program that provides a way to search for specific information on the World Wide Web, such as Yahoo!.

selection   Text or a pictures that the author has highlighted so that the next action the author performs affects only the highlighted text or picture(s).

server   A computer on a network, used to store information and "serve" it to other computers that contact it through the network. A Web server stores Web pages, which it serves to the browsers that tap it through the Internet.

shareware   Software programs that users are permitted to acquire and evaluate for free. Shareware is different from freeware in that, if a person likes the shareware program and plans to use it on a regular basis, he or she is expected to send a fee to the programmer.

signature   A block of text on a Web page, usually near the bottom, that identifies the page's author or the Web master. Signatures often include a mailto link to the author's email address.

surfing   Another term for **browsing** the Internet.

symbol   A character that's not on the keyboard, such as a copyright symbol. In FrontPage Express, you add symbols to your pages from a special dialog box.

table   A box or grid used to arrange text or pictures in neat rows and columns.

tag   A code in the HTML language.

title   The name that identifies a particular Web page. A Web page's title appears in the title bar at the very top of the browser window.

toolbar   In a program, a row of icons or buttons, usually near the top of the program's window, you can click to perform common tasks.

undo   A feature of FrontPage Express and some other programs that enables you to reverse an action you performed, if you change your mind. You can reverse several actions.

upload The act of copying information to a server computer from your computer. **See also** download.

URL Short for **Uniform Resource Locator**. A method of standardizing the addresses of different types of Internet resources so that they can all be accessed easily from within a Web browser.

Web **See** World Wide Web.

Web site A group of individual Web pages linked together into a single, multi-page document. A Web site is sometimes used to describe a whole Web server, or all pages on a particular domain.

Webmaster The person responsible for the management and maintenance of a particular Web page or Web site. This person is sometimes (but not always) the Web page author.

WinZIP A Windows program used to compress files into archives so that they can be uploaded or downloaded more quickly and conveniently. Also used to decompress files later to restore them to their original state.

wizard Automated routines, used throughout Windows, for conveniently performing a step-by-step procedure, such as setting up Windows or configuring it for the Internet.

World Wide Web (WWW or Web) A set of Internet computers and services that provides an easy-to-use system for finding information and moving among resources.

Yahoo! A popular search engine.

Index

A

active links, 70
adding
  animated GIFs, 90
  borders
    pictures, 82
    tables, 101
  captions to tables, 100
  horizontal lines, 72
  links to tables, 98
  paragraphs, HTML, 144
  picture backgrounds, 88-89
  pictures
    with HTML, 142-143
    to tables, 98-99
    to Web pages, 79
  special characters, 35
  symbols, 35
  tables, 96
  text, 34, 97
  URLs to ads/letterhead, 132
  Web sites to search engines, 126
addresses (Web)
  adding to ads/letterhead, 132
  copying, 53
  links, 52, 54-55
  publishing Web pages, 116
Align Left button, 42
Align Right button, 42
aligning
  horizontal lines, 73
  paragraphs, 42
  pictures, 83
  table text, 97
  text with pictures, 84

anchors, 60-61
animated GIFs, 90
appearance
  forms, 107
  horizontal lines, 73
Appearance tab (Image Properties dialog box), 82
archives, 155
attributes (HTML), 144

B

background
  colors, 70-71
  pictures, 78, 88-89
  sound, 92-93
  tables, 103
Background tab (Page Properties dialog box), 70-71
<body> tag, 139
Bold button, 47
bold text, 47
Bookmark command (Edit menu), 60
bookmarks, 60-61
borders
  colors, 102
  pictures, 82
  tables, 96, 101
browsers
  background sound support, 92
  default, 121
  font support, 45

Internet Explorer
  CD-ROM, ordering, 5
  downloading, 6-7
  installing, 4, 8-9
  updating, 7
  Web site, 5
  marquee support, 86
  multiple, viewing Web pages, 120-121
  viewing Web pages, 28-29, 119
Bulleted List button, 43
bulleted lists, 43
Bullets and Numbering command (Format menu), 44
buttons
  Align Left, 42
  Align Right, 42
  Bold, 47
  Bulleted List, 43
  Center, 42
  Copy, 38
  Create Hyperlink, 56, 85
  Cut, 39
  Decrease Indent, 41
  Decrease Text Size, 46
  Define Custom Colors, 48
  Edit Hyperlink, 56
  Increase Indent, 41
  Increase Text Size, 46
  Insert, 35
  Insert Image, 79, 98
  Italic, 47
  Numbered List, 43
  Paste, 38
  Text Color, 48
  Underline, 47

C

captions, tables, 100
carats (< >), HTML tags, 137
case sensitivity, HTML tags, 138
CD-ROMs
    clip art, 75
    Internet Explorer, ordering, 5
cells (tables)
    spacing, 101
    text, adding, 97
Center button, 42
character formatting, 32, 45
clip art, 74-75
Clip Art Connection Web site, 90
Close command (File menu), 24
closing Web pages, 24
color schemes, 70-71
colors
    background, 70-71
    custom, 71
    table borders, 102
    text, 48-49, 70-71
    transparent backgrounds, 78
columns (tables), 96
commands
    Edit menu
        Bookmark, 60
        Redo Clear, 37
        Undo Clear, 37
    File menu
        Close, 24
        Page Properties, 26
        Save, 23
    Format menu, Bullets and
      Numbering, 44
    Insert menu
        Horizontal Line, 72
        Marquee, 86
        Symbol, 35
    Table menu
        Insert Caption, 100
        Insert Table, 96
        Table Properties, 101
    Tools menu, Follow Hyperlink, 66
    View menu, HTML, 136
Composer, 151
**contact information (Web pages),
  19**
Copy button, 38
copying
    pictures, 75
    text, 38
    URLs, 53
Create Hyperlink button, 56, 85
Create Hyperlink dialog box, 85
cursors, 34
custom colors, 71
Cut button, 39
cutting and pasting text, 39

D

Decrease Indent button, 41
Decrease Text Size button, 46
default browser, 121
default colors, 71
Define Custom Colors button, 48
deleted text, recovering, 37
deleting text, 36
dialog boxes
    Create Hyperlink, 85
    Horizontal Line Properties, 73
    Image Properties, 82
    Marquee Properties, 87
    Page Properties
        Background tab, 70-71
        General tab, 92-93
    Saving, 6
    Table Properties
        background, 103
        border colors, 102
        borders, 101
digital pictures, 76
direction (marquees), 87
dividing pages, 72
domains, 122-123
Download.com Web site, 152
downloading
    files, links, 62-63
    FrontPage Express, 6-7
    Internet Explorer, 6-7
    programs, 154
    WinZip, 155

E

edit cursor, 34
Edit Hyperlink button, 56
Edit menu commands
    Bookmark, 60
    Redo Clear, 37
    Undo Clear, 37
editing
    link sources, 54
    text, 33
    titles, 26
    Web pages, 118
email
    links
        creating, 64-65
        sending, 133
    Web site publicity, 133
Excite directory, adding Web sites,
  130
Excite Web site, 74
extracting files, 155

F

feedback, receiving, 20
fields (forms), 104
File menu commands
    Close, 24
    Page Properties, 26
    Save, 23

filenames, 16
files
    archives, 155
    downloading links, creating, 62-63
    extracting, 155
    ie5setup.exe, 6-7
    local, 121
    size, 63
    storing, 59
    unzipping, 154-155
    Wave, 91
    zip, 154-155
finding
    animted GIFs, 90
    background pictures, 88
    bookmarked text, 61
    clip art, 74
    FrontPage Express, 5
    graphics programs, 152-153
    pictures, 74
    server information, 112
    server space, 110-111
    sound clips, 91
    Web authoring programs, 148-149
    Web authoring tools, 152-153
    Web site promotion places, 126-127
Follow Hyperlink command (Tools
  menu), 66
fonts, 45
Form Page Wizard, 104-107
Format menu commands, Bullets
  and Numbering, 44
Format toolbar, 11

formatting
    links, 56-57
    lists, 43
    paragraphs, 40
    tables
        pictures, 99
        text, 97
    text, 32, 144
forms
    appearance, 107
    creating, 104-107
    fields, 104
Forms toolbar, 11
FrontPage, 150
FrontPage Express
    already installed, checking, 4
    closing Web pages, 24
    downloading, 6-7
    finding on Microsoft Web site, 5
    HTML, 139
    installing, 8-9
    opening, 10
    Personal Home Page Wizard
        contact information, 19
        information order, 21
        items to include on pages, 15
        link styles, 17
        naming pages, 16
        personal information, 18
        producing Web pages, 22
        receiving feedback choices, 20
        starting, 14
    toolbars, 11
    ToolTips, 11
    Web pages
        opening, 24-25
        saving, 23-24

G

General tab (Page Properties
dialog box), 92-93
GeoCities Web site, 111
GIFs, animated, 90
graphics programs, 152-153

H

\<h1\> tag, 137
handles, 80
\<head\> tag, 138
Heading styles, 40
height, horizontal lines, 73
help
Internet Explorer, 9
Paint, 76
ToolTips, 11
hiding toolbars, 11
Horizontal Line command (Insert
menu), 72
Horizontal Line Properties dialog
box, 73
horizontal lines
adding, 72
appearance, 73
host requirements, 111
HTML (Hypertext Markup
Language), 136
attributes, 144
FrontPage Express, 139
overview, 136-137

pictures, adding, 142-143
source code
error checking, 141
viewing, 136, 140-141
tags, 134, 137, 145
\<body\>, 139
carats (\< \>), 137
case sensitivity, 138
\<h1\>, 137
\<head\>, 138
\<IMG SRC=\>, 143
\<p\>, 144
\<title\>, 139
text formatting, 144
undoing coding, 143
Web pages, creating, 138-141
HTML command (View menu),
136
Hypertext Markup Language. See
HTML

I - K

ie5setup.exe, 6-7
Image Properties dialog box, 82
images. See pictures
\<IMG SRC=\> tag, 143
importing links, 17
Increase Indent button, 41
Increase Text Size button, 46
indenting paragraphs, 41
InformIT Web site, 156-157
Insert button, 35
Insert Caption command (Table
menu), 100

Insert Image button, 79, 98
Insert menu commands
Horizontal Line, 72
Marquee, 86
Symbol, 35
Insert Table command (Table
menu), 96
installing
FrontPage Express, 8-9
Internet Explorer, 4, 8-9
interactive forms, 104-107
Internet, viewing Web pages,
119-121
Internet Explorer
CD-ROM, 5
downloading, 6-7
installing, 4, 8-9
updating, 7
Web site, 5
ISPs (Internet service providers),
110
Italic button, 47
italic text, 47

L

lines (horizontal)
adding, 72
appearance, 73
link sources, 52
editing, 54
pictures as, 57
linking
specific place on pages, 60-61
Web pages, 58-59

links, 52-53
active, 70
creating, 56-57
email, 64-65
file downloads, creating, 62-63
formatting, 56-57
importing, 17
mailto, 64-65
navigation menu, 58-59
permission, 55
pictures as, 85
sending via email, 133
sources, 52
editing, 54
pictures as, 57
styles, 17
tables, 98
testing, 66-67
URLs, 52, 54-55
visited, 70
List styles, 40
listing Web sites
Excite directory, 130
Yahoo! directory, 128-129
lists
bulleted, 43
creating, 43
numbered, 43
styles, 44
local files, 121

M

**Macmillan Web Publishing
resources Web site, 145**
Macmillan Web site, 54
mailto links, 64-65
**Marquee command (Insert
menu), 86**
Marquee Properties dialog box, 87
marquees
browser support, 86
text, 87
Times Square–style, 86-87
Microsoft
FrontPage, 150
FrontPage Express
already installed, checking, 4
closing Web pages, 24
downloading, 6-7
finding on Microsoft Web site, 5
HTML, 139
installing, 8-9
opening, 10
opening Web pages, 24-25
Personal Home Page Wizard. See
Personal Home Page Wizard
saving Web pages, 23-24
toolbars, 11
ToolTips, 11
MSDN Web Workshop Web site,
156
Paint
creating pictures, 76-77
transparent backgrounds, 78
Web site, Internet Explorer page, 5
moving
pictures, 79
text, 39

N - O

naming
mailto links, 65
Web pages, 16
navigation menu, 58-59
Netscape Composer, 151
**Netscape Developer's Edge Web
site, 156**
Network Solutions Web site, 122
Normal style, 40
Notepad, HTML source code, 141
Numbered List button, 43
numbered lists, 43

offline Web page testing, 121
opening. *See also* **starting**
FrontPage Express, 10
local files, 121
Web pages, 24-25

P - Q

<p> tag, 144
**Page Properties command (File
menu), 26**
Page Properties dialog box
Background tab, 70-71
General tab, 92-93
Paint
creating pictures, 76-77
transparent backgrounds, 78

paragraph formatting, 32, 40
paragraphs
  aligning, 42
  indenting, 41
  styles, 40
passwords (publishing), 117
Paste button, 38-39
pasting text, 38-39
Personal Home Page Wizard
  contact information, 19
  information order, 21
  items to include on pages, 15
  link styles, 17
  naming pages, 16
  personal information, 18
  producing pages, 22
  receiving feedback choices, 20
  starting, 14
personal information (Web pages), 18
pictures
  adding
    with HTML, 142-143
    to tables, 98-99
    to Web pages, 79
  aligning, 83
  as backgrounds, 88-89
  borders, 82
  copying from Web, 75
  creating, 76-77

  finding, 74
  link sources, 52, 57
  as links, 85
  moving, 79
  shaping, 81
  sizing, 80
  spacing, 82
  table backgrounds, 103
  text alignment with, 84
  transparent backgrounds, 78
playing background sound, 92-93
preparations (publishing), 113
programs
  downloading, 154
  graphics, 152-153
  multiple browser, 120-121
  Web authoring
    finding, 148-149
    Microsoft FrontPage, 150
    Microsoft FrontPage Express. *See*
      FrontPage Express
    Netscape Composer, 151
  WinZip, 155
promoting Web sites, 126-127
publicizing Web sites, 132
  email, 133
  Excite directory, 130
  places, finding, 126-127
  submission services, 131
  Yahoo! directory, 128-129

publishing Web pages
  domains, 122-123
  edited, 118
  file storage, 59
  host requirements, 111
  multiple browser testing, 120-121
  offline testing, 121
  passwords, 117
  preparations, 113
  server information, 112
  server space, finding, 110-111
  testing, 119
  URLs, 116
  Web Publishing Wizard, 114-117
  updated, 118

R

re-opening Web pages, 24
receiving feedback, 20
recording sound clips, 91
recovering deleted text, 37
Redo Clear command (Edit menu), 37
registering domains, 123
republishing Web pages, 118
resizing pictures, 80
rows (tables), 96

S

Save command (File menu), 23
Saving dialog box, 6
saving Web pages, 23
scrolling marquees, 86-87
search engines, adding Web sites,
  126
selecting
  background colors, 70-71
  default browser, 121
  link URLs, 54-55
  list styles, 44
  paragraph styles, 40
  table background, 103
  text, 32
      color, 48-49, 70-71
      fonts, 45
sending links via email, 133
servers
  host requirements, 111
  information, 112
  space, finding, 110-111
shaping pictures, 81
Shareware.com Web site, 152
signatures, 64-65
sites (Web)
  adding to search engines, 126
  Clip Art Connection, 90
  description, 129
  Download.com, 152
  Excite, 74
  GeoCities, 111
  InformIT, 156-157
  Internet Explorer, 5

linking pages, 58-59
listing in Excite directory, 130
listing in Yahoo! directory, 128-129
Macmillan, 54
Macmillan Web Publishing resources,
  145
Microsoft
  FrontPage, 150
  Internet Explorer page, 5
  MSDN Web Workshop, 156
Netscape Composer, 151
Netscape Developer's Edge, 156
Network Solutions, 122
promoting, 126-127
publicizing, 132
  email, 133
  Excite directory, 130
  places, finding, 126-127
  submission services, 131
  Yahoo! directory, 128-129
publishing
  domains, 122-123
  edited, 118
  file storage, 59
  host requirements, 111
  multiple browser testing, 120-121
  offline testing, 121
  passwords, 117
  preparations, 113
  server information, 112
  server space, finding, 110-111
  testing, 119
  URLs, 116
  Web Publishing Wizard, 114-117
  updated, 118

Shareware.com, 152
submission services, 131
Talk City, 111
TUCOWS library, 149
updating, 115
WinZip, 155
Yahoo!, 74
sizing
  borders, 82
  columns (tables), 96
  files, downloading links, 63
  pictures, 80
  rows (tables), 96
  text, 46
sound (background), 92-93
sound clips, 91
source code (HTML), 140-141
sources (links), 52
  editing, 54
  pictures as, 57
spacing
  pictures, 82
  table cells, 101
special characters, 35
speed
  marquees, 87
  picture backgrounds, 89
Standard toolbar, 11
starting. *See also* **opening**
  blank pages, 27
  Form Page Wizard, 104
  Personal Home Page Wizard, 14
  Web Publishing Wizard, 114
storing files, 59

styles
  links, 17
  lists, 44
  paragraphs, 40
submission services, 131
Submissions software, 131
**Symbol command (Insert menu),
  35**
symbols, 35

T

Table menu commands
  Insert Caption, 100
  Insert Table, 96
  Table Properties, 101
**Table Properties command (Table
  menu), 101**
Table Properties dialog box
  background, 103
  border colors, 102
  borders, 101
tables
  background, 103
  borders, 96
    adding, 101
    color, 102
  captions, 100
  cells
    spacing, 101
    text, adding, 97
  creating, 96

  links, 98
  pictures, 98-99
  text, 97
tags (HTML), 134, 137, 145
  attributes, 144
  <body>, 139
  carats (< >), 137
  case sensitivity, 138
  <h1>, 137
  <head>, 138
  <IMG SRC=>, 143
  <p>, 144
  <title>, 139
Talk City Web site, 111
targets, 60-61
testing
  links, 66-67
  Web pages, 119
    multiple browsers, 120-121
    offline, 121
text
  adding, 34, 97
  bold, 47
  bookmarked, finding, 61
  color, 48-49, 70-71
  copying, 38
  deleted, recovering, 37
  deleting, 36
  editing, 33
  fonts, 45
  HTML formatting, 144
  italic, 47
  link sources, 52
  links, formatting, 56-57

TUCOWS library Web site

  lists, 43-44
  marquees, 87
  moving, 39
  paragraphs
    adding (HTML), 144
    aligning, 42
    indenting, 41
    style, selecting, 40
  picture alignment, 84
  selecting, 32
  sizing, 46
  special characters, 35
  symbols, 35
  underlined, 47
Text Color button, 48
**Times Square-style marquee,
  86-87**
title tag, 139
titles, 16, 26
toolbars (FrontPage Express), 11
tools (Web authoring), 152-153
**Tools menu commands, Follow
  Hyperlink, 66**
ToolTips, 11
transparent backgrounds, 78
**troubleshooting HTML source
  code, 141**
TUCOWS library Web site, 149

U

Underline button, 47
underlining text, 47
Undo Clear command (Edit menu), 37
undoing
    HTML coding, 143
    mistakes, 37
    undos, 37
unzipping files, 154-155
updating
    Internet Explorer, 7
    Web pages, 118
    Web sites, 115
URLs (Uniform Resource Locators)
    adding to ads/letterhead, 132
    copying, 53
    links, 52, 54-55
    publishing Web pages, 116

V

View menu commands, HTML, 136
viewing
    animated GIFs, 90
    HTML source code, 136, 140-141
    toolbars, 11
    transparent backgrounds, 78
    Web pages, 119
        browsers, 28-29
        multiple browsers, 120-121
visited links, 70

W - Z

Wave files, 91
Web addresses. See URLs
Web authoring
    advanced techniques, learning, 156-157
    programs
        finding, 148-149
        Microsoft FrontPage, 150
        Microsoft FrontPage Express. See FrontPage Express
        Netscape Composer, 151
    tools, 2, 152-153
Web Publishing Wizard, 114-118
Web sites
    adding to search engines, 126
    Clip Art Connection, 90
    description, 129
    Download.com, 152
    Excite, 74
    GeoCities, 111
    InformIT, 156-157
    Internet Explorer, 5
    linking pages, 58-59
    listing in Excite directory, 130
    listing in Yahoo! directory, 128-129
    Macmillan, 54
    Macmillan Web Publishing resources, 145
    Microsoft
        FrontPage, 150
        Internet Explorer page, 5
        MSDN Web Workshop, 156

Netscape Composer, 151
Netscape Developer's Edge, 156
Network Solutions, 122
promoting, 126-127
publicizing, 132
    email, 133
    Excite directory, 130
    places, finding, 126-127
    submission services, 131
    Yahoo! directory, 128-129
publishing
    domains, 122-123
    edited, 118
    file storage, 59
    host requirements, 111
    multiple browser testing, 120-121
    offline testing, 121
    passwords, 117
    preparations, 113
    server information, 112
    server space, finding, 110-111
    testing, 119
    URLs, 116
    Web Publishing Wizard, 114-117
    updated, 118
Shareware.com, 152
submission services, 131
Talk City, 111
TUCOWS library, 149
updating, 115
WinZip, 155
Yahoo!, 74

width, horizontal lines, 73
WinZip, 155
wizards
    Form Page, 104-107
    Personal Home Page
        contact information, 19
        information order, 21
        items to include on pages, 15
        link styles, 17
        naming pages, 16
        personal information, 18
        producing pages, 22
        receiving feedback choices, 20
        starting, 14
    Web Publishing, 114-118

**Yahoo! directory, adding Web
  sites, 128-129**
Yahoo! Web site, 74

zip files, 154-155